# DAY HIKES IN
# Hawaii

♦

## 90 Great Hikes on
## KAUAI • MAUI • OAHU

Robert Stone

**Day Hike Books, Inc.**
RED LODGE, MONTANA

Published by Day Hike Books, Inc.
P.O. Box 865
Red Lodge, Montana 59068

Distributed by The Globe Pequot Press
246 Goose Lane
P.O. Box 480
Guilford, CT 06437-0480
800-243-0495 (direct order) · 800-820-2329 (fax order)
www.globe-pequot.com

Photographs by Robert Stone
Design by Paula Doherty

The author has made every attempt to provide accurate information in this book. However, trail routes and features may change—please use common sense and forethought, and be mindful of your own capabilities. Let this book guide you, but be aware that each hiker assumes responsibility for their own safety. The author and publisher do not assume any responsibility for loss, damage, or injury caused through the use of this book.

Cover photo: Waimea Canyon, Kauai Hikes 2—8
Back cover photo: Hana—Waianapanapa Coastal Trail,
Maui Hike 27

# Table of Contents

## Kauai

# Maui

# Oahu

# Kauai

## PAGES 9–79

# Island of Kauai

Some of the finest hikes in all Hawaii and possibly the world are found on the island of Kauai. From precarious cliffs to relaxing strolls along bayside beaches, these 30 day hikes offer the hiker excellent possibilities to explore and enrich their time spent on Kauai.

All levels of hiking experience are accommodated in this guide, with an emphasis on outstanding scenery and memorable features. Each hike includes a map, detailed driving and hiking directions, and a summary. An overall map of Kauai and the locations of hikes is found on pages 14—15.

The verdant "Garden Isle" of Kauai is an emerald green gem of lush foliage, cascading waterfalls, dramatic valleys, and canyons. The 553-square-mile island of Kauai is Hawaii's oldest and northernmost island. Mount Waialeale, the wettest place on earth, averages 451 inches of rain annually. It is the source of Kauai's seven major rivers and many of its waterfalls. Nearly half of the 335,000-acre island is mountainous forest, accessible only by its hiking trails.

To help you decide which hikes are most appealing to you, a brief summary of the highlights is included with each hike. You may enjoy these areas for a short time or the whole day. Reference the overall map to locate the general location of the hikes.

Polihale State Park is a two-mile strip of sandy beach on the dry west coast of Kauai. The park's sheer, majestic grey cliffs and jagged peaks rise above the wide stretch of white sand and the deep blue ocean beyond. The park has picnic facilities and is an ideal spot for viewing sunsets. Hike 1 is a beach stroll through this state park.

The colossal Waimea Canyon, known as the Grand Canyon of the Pacific, is ten miles in length with glowing jewel-colored cathedral walls that descend 3,000 feet. The cool, wet high country of Kokee State Park, adjacent to Waimea Canyon, is a lush 4,300-acre wilderness preserve with more than 40 miles of hiking trails and freshwater streams. The trails wind through the forest and along the canyon rim. There are 7 hikes found in the canyon and Kokee area (see page 18).

Along the dry, sunny south coast of Kauai are the white sand beaches of Poipu—Hikes 9 and 10. These beaches are an excellent place to spend the day beachcombing, exploring tide-pools and promontories, and enjoying the water. Pools, blow-holes, off-shore reefs, and coves are here to discover from either land or water.

The Wailua River watershed flows through a lush valley to the island's east coast. Beautiful forests and waterfalls are highlights for the 10 hikes that lie throughout the valley. Wailua Falls and Opaekaa Falls are two of the lovelier waterfalls. For a magnificent hike to the interior of the island, try the Powerline Trail (Hikes 11 and 25).

Along the tropical north shore are quaint one-lane bridges, rainbows and serene villages with weathered houses, flowering gardens, and overgrown hedges of hibiscus and plumeria. Crescent-shaped beaches lie nestled between tall sea cliffs and waterfalls drop into picture-perfect pools. (See the north coast hikes, page 58). On the northernmost point of Kauai is the 52-foot Kilauea Lighthouse, built in 1913 and now within the Kilauea National Wildlife Refuge. The lighthouse sits on a peninsula that offers a great vantage point for observing birds, seals, dolphins, sea turtles, and humpback whales.

Na Pali State Park on the northwest coast of Kauai is home to the awesome Na Pali coastline, with primeval emerald green valleys and imposing perpendicular cliffs plunging 4,000 feet to the cobalt blue Pacific. The state park, which takes in 6,000 acres, is accessible only by foot or boat. The Kalalau Trail hugs the coastline while winding along these cliffs in Kalalau Valley (Hikes 29 and 30).

If you have little time to hike but still want to enjoy a few trails, try the Pihea Trail (Hike 2), the scalloped beaches on the south coast (Hikes 9 and 10) and the Kalalau Trail along the Na Pali Coast (Hikes 29 and 30). These hikes offer some of the most beautiful and incredible scenery found in Kauai.

Getting around Kauai is easy. All of the hikes are accessed via the main highway that lies along the perimeter of the island—Highway 50 or Highway 56, depending on your direction out of Lihue. The highway markers roughly correspond with mileage distances in each direction beginning in Lihue at mile marker "0." The Waimea Canyon/Kokee trailheads are right off Kokee Road, the main access road for the parks. All of the hikes are an hour's drive or less from anywhere on the island. Be cautious, however, of unpaved roads. Their conditions can change rapidly because of frequent rainfalls.

Be prepared with appropriate hiking attire and a few necessities. Wear supportive, comfortable hiking shoes. (They will likely get muddy.) Wet rain forests to dry deserts will make it necessary to have a variety of clothing when exploring Kauai. Be sure to bring a hat and rain jacket. Sunscreen, inset repellent, sunglasses, drinking water, and snacks are a must. Don't forget swimwear and outdoor gear to use at the coast.

Enjoy the trails and scenery! Your day will be enhanced with a hike in Kauai's beautiful landscape.

# Waimea Canyon and Kokee State Park

Waimea Canyon and the Kokee State Park area are referred to as the "Grand Canyon of the Pacific." The canyon measures ten miles long by one mile wide, with a depth of 3,000 feet. Sheer cliffs and multicolored canyon walls with cascading waterfalls are typical views. The Kokee area adjacent to the canyon includes everything from high mountain peaks that overlook the sea to atmospheric swampy landscapes dripping with lush vegetation.

Hikes 2—8 explore this exquisite area of the island. These 7 hikes offer an excellent cross-section of all that these state parks have to offer. The views into this ancient and richly colored canyon highlight the layers of black, red, purple, and pink rock framed by the changing cloud formations. These selected hikes have a variety of scenic overlooks into the canyon, deep jungle trails with lush vegetation, streams, waterfalls, and swimming pools. Wild pigs and goats may be spotted on any of the hikes.

Kokee State Park, north of Waimea Canyon, lies on a cool plateau with quiet forests and excellent vantage points for viewing the northwest coast from afar. Trails lead through thick, shady jungles teeming with the songs of birds. The area has a lodge with cabin rentals and a restaurant. Next to the lodge is the Kokee Natural History Museum, a superb facility offering everything you would want to know about the area, plus a gift shop with books and maps.

A map of the canyon and park is found on page 19.

# Kauai
## MAP OF THE HIKES

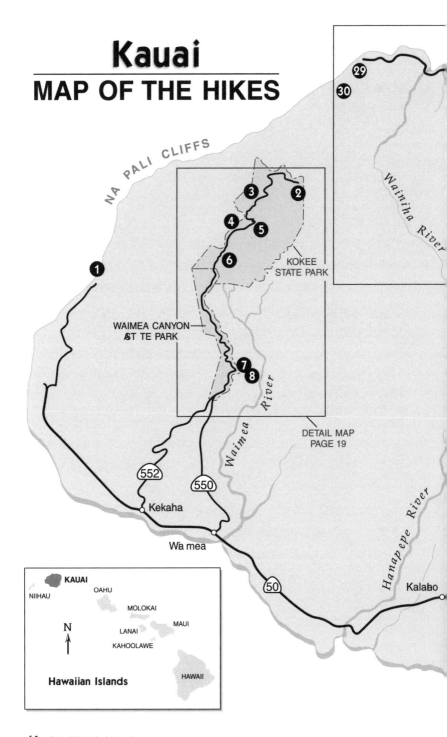

NA PALI CLIFFS

Wainiha River

**3** **2**
**4** **5**
**6**
KOKEE
STATE PARK

**1**

WAIMEA CANYON
STE PARK

**7**
**8**
River

DETAIL MAP
PAGE 19

Waimea River

552
550
Kekaha
Wa mea

Hanapepe River

50
Kalaho

**29**
**30**

KAUAI

NIIHAU   OAHU

MOLOKAI

N   LANAI   MAUI

KAHOOLAWE

Hawaiian Islands   HAWAII

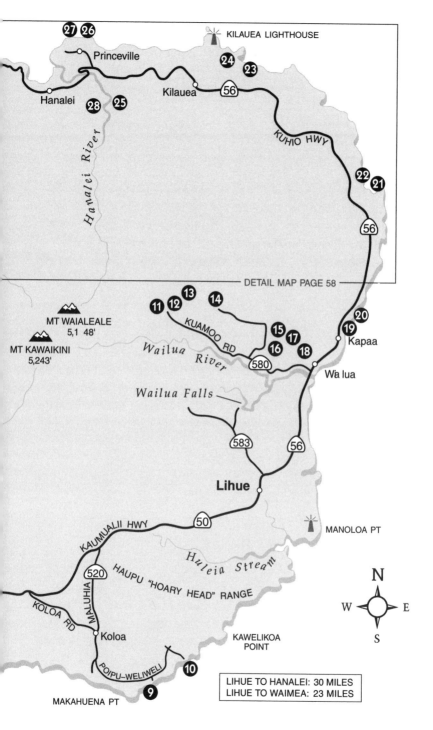

KILAUEA LIGHTHOUSE

KAUAI

Princeville

Hanalei

Kilauea

KUHIO HWY

56

DETAIL MAP PAGE 58

MT WAIALEALE
5,1 48'

MT KAWAIKINI
5,243'

Wailua River

KUAMOO RD

580

Kapaa

Wa lua

Wailua Falls

583

56

Lihue

50

KAUMUALII HWY

MANOLOA PT

Huleia Stream

520

HAUPU "HOARY HEAD" RANGE

MALUHIA

KOLOA RD

Koloa

KAWELIKOA
POINT

POIPU-WELIWELI

MAKAHUENA PT

N
W — E
S

LIHUE TO HANALEI: 30 MILES
LIHUE TO WAIMEA: 23 MILES

# Hike 1
## Polihale State Park and Beach

**Hiking distance:** 0.5 to 4 miles round trip
**Hiking time:** 1 to 3 hours
**Elevation gain:** Level
**Maps:** U.S.G.S. Makaha Point
        Earthwalk Press Northwestern Kauai Recreation Map

**Summary of hike:** Polihale State Park is a remote 140-acre park at the end of the road on the western end of Kauai. The park offers access to 15 miles of uninterrupted sand beach from Polihale Ridge, at the southwest end of the Na Pali cliffs, to Kekaha Beach Park. This hike follows the long sandy strand from the base of the spectacular Na Pali peaks to Barking Sands Beach by the Pacific Missile Range Facility. The islands of Niihau and Lehua are visible across the channel. Facilities include restrooms, showers, picnic shelters, and campsites.

**Driving directions:** From Lihue, drive 39 miles west on Highway 50 to the end of the highway, seven miles past the town of Kekaha. Shortly after the Pacific Missile Range Facility, the road forks. Take the fork to the right (east) for 0.5 miles to the first left turn. Turn left, as the sign directs, onto a cane field road. Continue 1.8 miles to the end of the road and turn left. Drive toward the ocean 3.1 miles to the Polihale day use parking area. Turn left and park.

**Hiking directions:** From the parking area, walk towards the ocean. Begin to the right, exploring the forbidding, vertical Na Pali cliffs. On the slopes, hidden in the brush at the edge of the cliffs, are the remains of an ancient *heiau* (temple). Now head left on the long expanse of isolated beach that stretches for miles. The back end of the beach is bordered by massive dunes, reaching as high as 100 feet at Nohili Point. Follow the coastline southwest towards Barking Sands Beach and the sand dunes. The Pacific Missile Range Facility is two miles down the beach, which you cannot miss. It is a good turnaround spot.

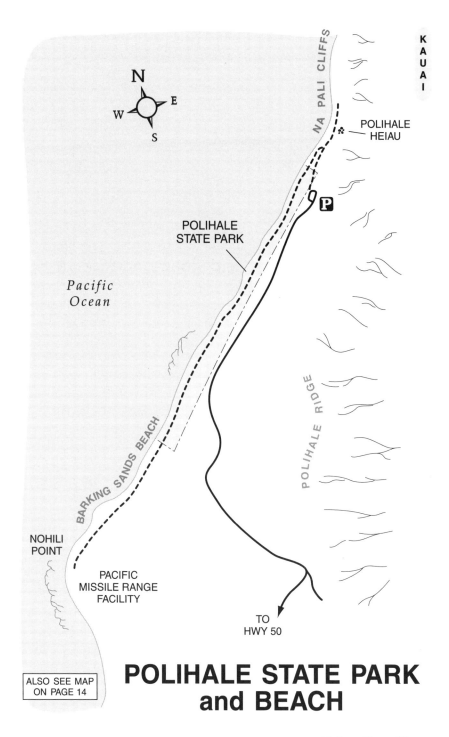

**N** E W S

K A U A I

NA PALI CLIFFS

POLIHALE
HEIAU

P

POLIHALE
STATE PARK

*Pacific
Ocean*

POLIHALE RIDGE

BARKING SANDS BEACH

NOHILI
POINT

PACIFIC
MISSILE RANGE
FACILITY

TO
HWY 50

ALSO SEE MAP
ON PAGE 14

# POLIHALE STATE PARK
## and BEACH

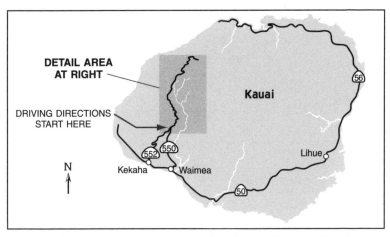

DETAIL AREA AT RIGHT

DRIVING DIRECTIONS START HERE

Kauai

56

N

550
552
Kekaha    Waimea

Lihue

50

# Waimea Canyon and Kokee State Park
## Hikes 2—8

Driving directions for hikes 2 through 8 begin from the junction in Waimea Canyon where Waimea Canyon Drive/Highway 550 and Kokee Road/Highway 552 merge (indicated by the arrow). To arrive at this junction, follow these directions:

### FROM LIHUE, TWO ROUTES LEAD TO THIS JUNCTION:

**ROUTE 1.** Drive 23 miles southwest on Highway 50 to Waimea Canyon Drive/Highway 550 in the town of Waimea, just beyond mile marker 23. Turn right and drive 6.7 miles to the junction where the road merges with Kokee Road/Highway 552.

**ROUTE 2.** Drive 26.5 miles southwest on Highway 50 to Alae Road (which becomes Kokee Road/Highway 552) in the town of Kekaha. The well-signed turnoff is between mile markers 26 and 27. Turn right and drive 7.6 miles to the junction where the road merges with Waimea Canyon Drive/Highway 550.

Due to the frequency of rain in this area, it is not advisable to drive on unpaved roads with two-wheel drive vehicles. Doing so could lead to a "day hike" back to civilization. Check with the Kokee Lodge or the Kokee Natural History Museum to find out current road conditions.

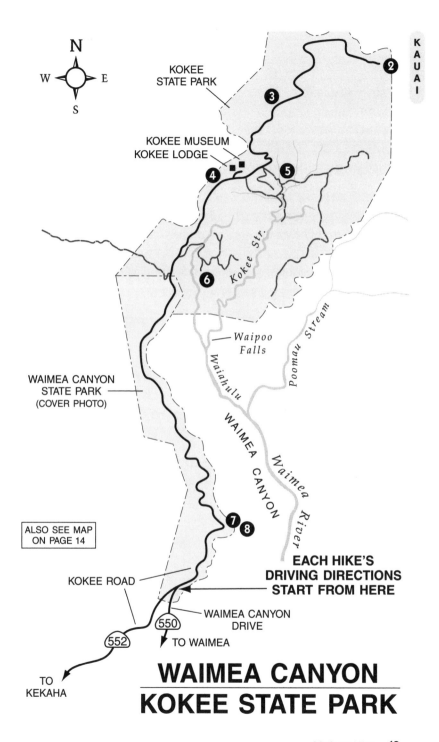

N
W   E
S

KOKEE
STATE PARK

KAUAI

**2**

**3**

KOKEE MUSEUM
KOKEE LODGE

**4**    **5**

*Kokee Str.*

**6**

*Waipoo Falls*

*Poomau Stream*

*Waiahulu*

WAIMEA CANYON
STATE PARK
(COVER PHOTO)

WAIMEA CANYON

*Waimea River*

ALSO SEE MAP
ON PAGE 14

**7 8**

**EACH HIKE'S
DRIVING DIRECTIONS
START FROM HERE**

KOKEE ROAD

(550)

WAIMEA CANYON
DRIVE

(552)

TO WAIMEA

TO
KEKAHA

# WAIMEA CANYON
# KOKEE STATE PARK

# Hike 2
# Pihea Trail

**Hiking distance:** 3.5 miles round trip
**Hiking time:** 2 hours
**Elevation gain:** 450 feet
**Maps:** U.S.G.S. Haena
    Trails of Kokee State Park map
    Earthwalk Press Northwestern Kauai Recreation Map

**Summary of hike:** The Pihea Trail is among the premier hiking paths in the Kokee/Waimea Canyon area. The trail traverses the narrow ridge in the Na Pali Kona Forest Reserve between the Kalalau Valley, the largest valley along the Na Pali cliffs, and the Alakai Swamp. The views extend 4,000 feet down the mossy, fluted cliffs of the Kalalau Valley, which drops sharply into the ocean. The views inland extend over layers of folded forested canyons and ridges to Mount Waialeale, the wettest spot on earth with an average of 451 inches of annual rainfall. Alakai Swamp is an incredible, atmospheric area like nowhere else.

**Driving directions:** From the junction of Waimea Canyon Drive and Kokee Road in Waimea Canyon (directions to junction on page 18) drive 8.7 miles up the winding canyon to the Kokee Lodge and museum on the left. Continue 3.8 miles past the museum turnoff to the Pihea Trail parking lot at the road's end.

**Hiking directions:** Take the paved path a short distance to the 4,280-foot Puu O Kila Lookout. After marveling at the views, follow the edge of the cliffs downhill on the wet erod-ed path, crossing large red rock slabs. The path is usually muddy and slippery. Continue over numerous rises, dips, and several short boardwalks along the rim of the Kalalau Valley. The panoramic, everchanging views are stunning. At 1.1 miles, the path reaches a junction near Pihea Peak. The short, steep spur trail veers left to Pihea Vista. Continue on the main trail, leaving the rim of Kalalau Valley. Descend southeast, skirting the bogs into the forbidding Alakai Swamp, a very large bog at the foot of Mount Waialeale. Boardwalks allow easy access into the swampy atmosphere. At 1.75 miles, the trail intersects the Alakai Swamp Trail. This is our turnaround spot.

To hike further, both the Pihea Trail and the Alakai Swamp Trail continue downhill to Mohihi Road at 3.7 miles.

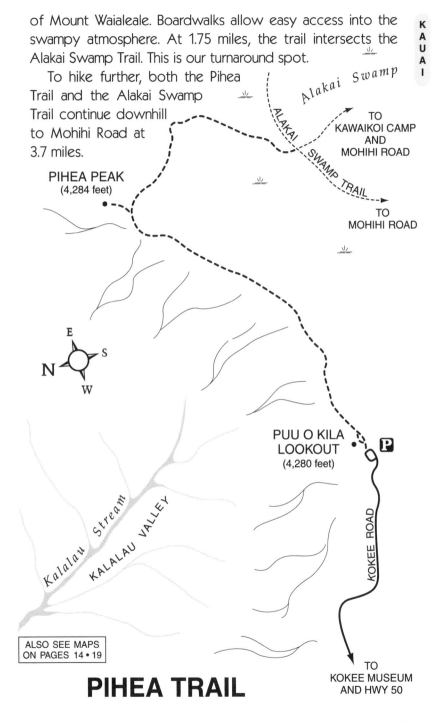

Alakai Swamp

ALAKAI SWAMP TRAIL

TO
KAWAIKOI CAMP
AND
MOHIHI ROAD

TO
MOHIHI ROAD

PIHEA PEAK
(4,284 feet)

E
N — S
W

PUU O KILA
LOOKOUT
(4,280 feet)

P

Kalalau Stream

KALALAU VALLEY

KOKEE ROAD

ALSO SEE MAPS
ON PAGES 14 • 19

TO
KOKEE MUSEUM
AND HWY 50

# PIHEA TRAIL

# Hike 3
# Awaawapuhi Trail

**Hiking distance:** 6.5 miles round trip
**Hiking time:** 3.5 hours
**Elevation gain:** 1,600 feet
**Maps:** U.S.G.S. Haena and Makaha Point
  Trails of Kokee State Park

**Summary of hike:** This hike descends to the edge of the sheer cliffs and razor-edged ridges of the Nualolo and Awaawapuhi Valleys. There are inspiring panoramas of the steep, 3,000-foot vertical cliffs to the isolated Na Pali coast, accessible only by water. This trail can be combined with the Nualolo Trail (Hike 4) for a 9-mile loop hike. The two trails are connected by the Nualolo Cliffs Trail, a 2.2-mile connector trail that follows the rim of Nualolo Valley.

**Driving directions:** From the junction of Waimea Canyon Drive and Kokee Road in Waimea Canyon (directions to junction on page 18) drive 8.7 miles up the winding canyon to the Kokee Lodge and museum on the left. Continue 1.6 miles past the museum turnoff to the Awaawapuhi Trail parking lot on the left. It is located just beyond mile marker 17. Turn left and park.

**Hiking directions:** The trail begins on the south side of the parking lot and immediately enters the shade of the forest canopy. At a half mile, switchbacks descend through a lush, humid forest. Endemic trees and bushes are labeled along the way. At just under 2 miles, views open to the steep forested cliffs of the Awaawapuhi and Nualolo Valleys. There are several lookouts along the trail. At 3 miles is a junction with the Nualolo Cliffs Trail on the left. If you plan to return on the same path, stay to the right and continue on the Awaawapuhi Trail. In a quarter mile, the trail terminates at a metal railing, perched on the precarious ridge dividing the Awaawapuhi and Nualolo Valleys. The views extend from the steep, eroded cliffs 2,500 feet down to the ocean. Return by retracing your steps.

To hike the 9-mile loop, take the near-level Nualolo Cliffs Trail along the rim of the Na Pali cliffs for two miles to the Nualolo Cliffs Trail (Hike 4).

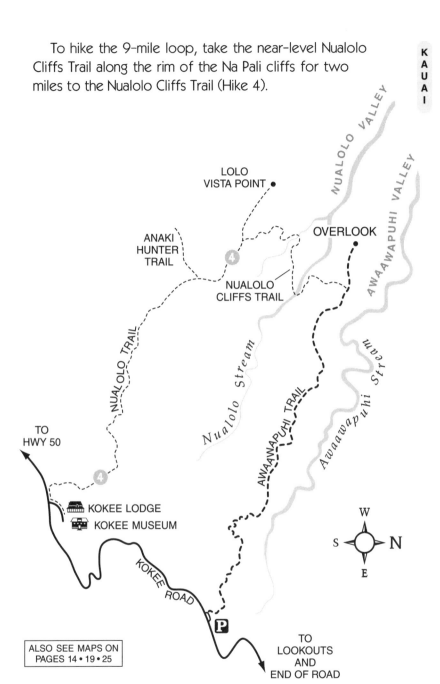

# AWAAWAPUHI TRAIL

# Hike 4
# Nualolo Cliffs Trail

**Hiking distance:** 7.5 miles round trip
**Hiking time:** 4 hours
**Elevation gain:** 1,600 feet
**Maps:** U.S.G.S. Haena and Makaha Point
  Trails of Kokee State Park

**Summary of hike:** This hike descends through a lush forest to panoramic vistas of the Na Pali coastline. The trail ends at Lolo Vista Point, a vertical perch 3,000 feet above the windswept cliffs of the Nualolo Valley. (If it is raining, this trail is not recommended, as several steep sections are dangerous.) This hike can be combined with the Awaawapuhi Trail (Hike 3) for a 9-mile loop hike. The two trails are connected by the Nualolo Cliffs Trail, a 2.2 mile connector trail with phenomenal views of the Na Pali coast. The Cliff Trail follows the rim's edge at the head of the Nualolo Valley, 3,000 feet above the ocean.

**Driving directions:** From the junction of Waimea Canyon Drive and Kokee Road in Waimea Canyon (directions to junction on page 18) drive 8.7 miles up the winding canyon to the Kokee Lodge and museum on the left. Turn left and park in the lot by the museum.

**Hiking directions:** Walk back down Kokee Road 50 yards to the signed trail on the right. Follow the trail sign a few yards to the right, reaching a signed footpath on the left. Short, steep switchbacks contour along the forested hillside. Cross over Kaunuohua Ridge, entering the Kuia Natural Area Reserve at 0.2 miles. Descend northwest through the dense forest for several miles. At 3 miles is a trail split. The Anaki Hunter Route bears left. Stay to the right, and steeply descend to a signed junction with the Nualolo Cliffs Trail at 3.4 miles. If you plan to return on the same path, stay to the left and continue on the Nualolo Cliffs Trail. The trail follows the southwest rim of the Nualolo Valley on an eroded slope. Pass numerous panoramic vistas to Lolo

Vista Point overlooking the dramatic valley.

To hike the 9-mile loop, take the near-level Nualolo Cliffs Trail along the rim of the Na Pali cliffs for two miles to a T-junction with the Awaawapuhi Trail (Hike 3).

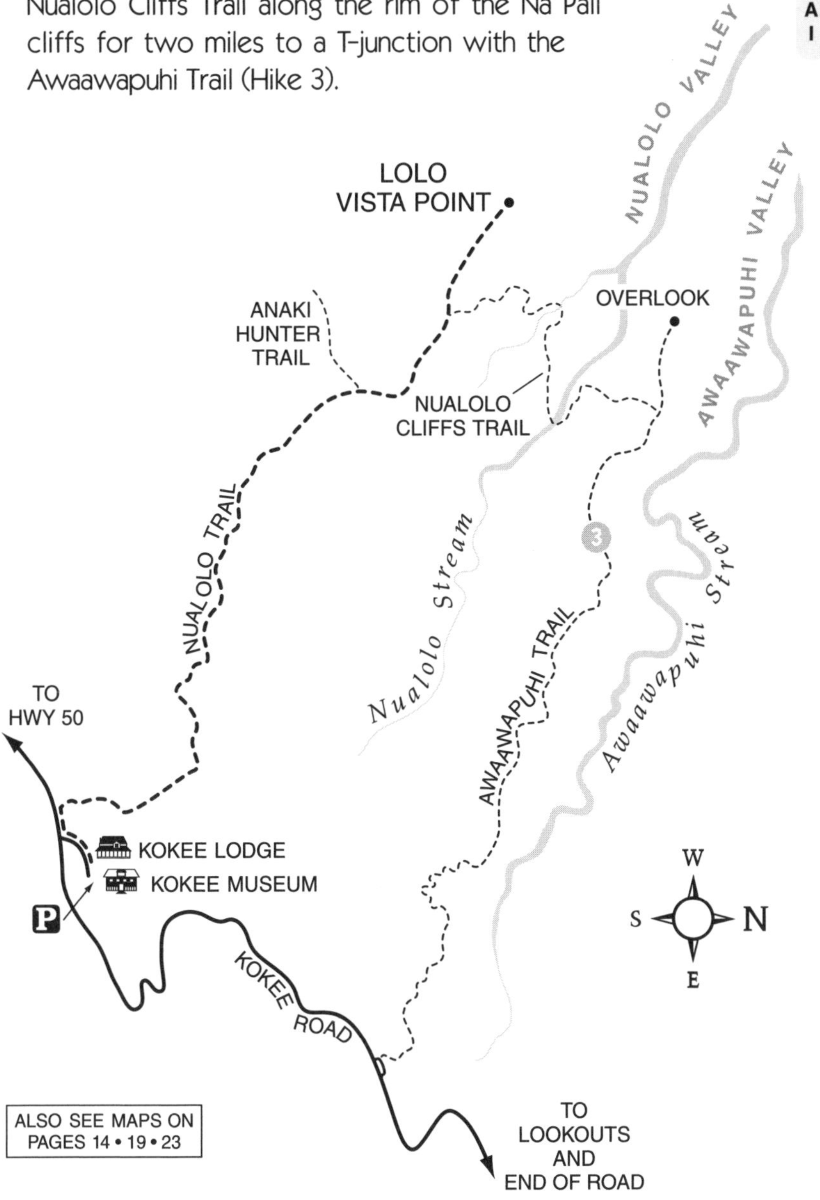

NUALOLO VALLEY

AWAAWAPUHI VALLEY

LOLO
VISTA POINT •

ANAKI
HUNTER
TRAIL

OVERLOOK •

NUALOLO
CLIFFS TRAIL

NUALOLO TRAIL

Nualolo Stream

Awaawapuhi Stream

③

AWAAWAPUHI TRAIL

TO
HWY 50

KOKEE LODGE
KOKEE MUSEUM

P

KOKEE ROAD

W

S ✦ N

E

TO
LOOKOUTS
AND
END OF ROAD

ALSO SEE MAPS ON
PAGES 14 • 19 • 23

# NUALOLO TRAIL

# Hike 5
# Puu Ka Ohelo—Berry Flat Loop

**Hiking distance:** 3.4 miles round trip
**Hiking time:** 1.5 hours
**Elevation gain:** 250 feet
**Maps:** U.S.G.S. Haena
Trails of Kokee State Park

**Summary of hike:** This loop hike winds through a dense, tropical jungle with large sugi pine groves and huge California redwoods that were planted in the 1930s. The picturesque jungle is profuse with plants, including red wavy grained koa, eucalyptus trees, strawberry guava trees, ginger, blackberries, and long rope-like vines.

**Driving directions:** From the junction of Waimea Canyon Drive and Kokee Road in Waimea Canyon (directions to junction on page 18) drive 8.7 miles up the winding canyon to the Kokee Lodge and museum on the left. Continue 0.3 miles past the museum turnoff to the Kokee Campground on the left. Turn left and park in the spaces on the left.

**Hiking directions:** Return to the Kokee Road, and walk 15 yards left to the signed Mohihi Road on the right. Take the unpaved road, immediately reaching a road fork. Bear left downhill on the forested road, crossing over Noe Stream to a T-junction at 0.4 miles. Bear left and cross over Elekeniiki Stream to a Y-fork at 0.7 miles. Begin the loop to the left on the Puu Ka Ohelo Trail. Head gradually uphill through the forest. Soon the trail levels off and winds through the shady forest canopy, crossing a few fallen trees to a signed junction. The Water Tank Trail bears left. Go right on the Berry Flat Trail. Wind through the lush forest, crossing the muddy headwaters of Elekeninui Stream. The footpath exits on Mohihi Road. Take the road to the right for a half mile, completing the loop. (Along the way, curve to the right at a road fork with the Kumuwela Road.) Return on the Mohihi Road to the campground.

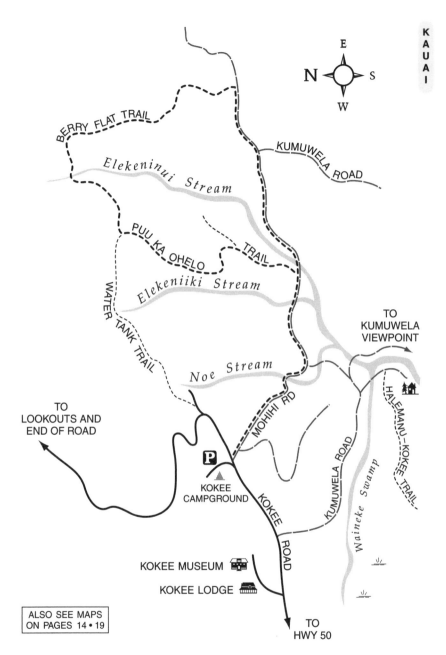

E
N ☀ S
W

BERRY FLAT TRAIL

KUMUWELA ROAD

*Elekeninui Stream*

PUU KA OHELO TRAIL

*Elekeniiki Stream*

WATER TANK TRAIL

*Noe Stream*

TO
KUMUWELA
VIEWPOINT

TO
LOOKOUTS AND
END OF ROAD

MOHIHI RD

HALEMANU–KOKEE TRAIL

**P**

KOKEE
CAMPGROUND

KUMUWELA ROAD

*Waineke Swamp*

KOKEE ROAD

KOKEE MUSEUM

KOKEE LODGE

ALSO SEE MAPS
ON PAGES 14 • 19

TO
HWY 50

# PUU KA OHELO–
# BERRY FLAT LOOP

# Hike 6
# Canyon Trail to Waipoo Falls

**Hiking distance:** 3.2 miles round trip
**Hiking time:** 1.5 hours
**Elevation gain:** 600 feet
**Maps:** U.S.G.S. Makaha Point, Haena and Waimea Canyon
      Trails of Kokee State Park

**Summary of hike:** Upper and Lower Waipoo Falls offer a cool retreat for hikers in Waimea Canyon. Upper Waipoo Falls is fronted by a large swimming pool set in a tropical garden. Lower Waipoo Falls has showering cascades and several small soaking pools. The trail begins at the head of Waimea Canyon and follows the canyon's north rim past several panoramic overlooks. A short detour on the Cliff Trail offers additional views into the canyon.

**Driving directions:** From the junction of Waimea Canyon Drive and Kokee Road in Waimea Canyon (directions to junction on page 18) drive 7.4 miles to Halemanu Road on the right. The road is located by the signed Cliff, Canyon and Black Pipe trailhead between mile markers 14 and 15. Parking is available on both sides of the road.

From Kokee Lodge and museum, drive 1.3 miles down canyon (south) to the trailhead.

**Hiking directions:** Hike down the unpaved Halemanu Road to the valley floor. Cross over Halemanu Stream and curve to the right. Ascend the hill to a signed junction at 0.6 miles. Leave the Halemanu Road, and take the right fork towards the Canyon Trail. The road soon becomes a footpath. Fifty yards ahead is a signed junction with the Cliff Trail. This short spur trail leads to an overlook of Waimea Canyon. Back on the Canyon Trail, descend down a steep narrow gorge along the Kokee irrigation ditch. Climb up a short hill to a vista of the multi-colored canyon walls and a signed junction. The left fork is the Black Pipe Trail. Take the right fork, staying on the Canyon Trail to an exposed, bare knoll overlooking the canyon. Pick up the trail at the lower edge of the knoll on the left. Head downhill along the eroded ridge, reaching a T-junction at Kokee Stream. Take the left fork upstream to Upper Waipoo Falls (Fall 1) and the pool. The main trail heads downstream to the two-tiered Lower Waipoo Falls (Fall 2). Return along the same trail.

To hike further, the Canyon Trail continues to Kumuwela Viewpoint.

*Waiahulu*

*Lower Waipoo Falls*

CANYON TRAIL

*Upper Waipoo Falls*

KNOLL

KUMUWELA VIEWPOINT

*Kokee Stream*

CANYON TRAIL

CLIFF VIEWPOINT

*Halemanu Stream*

BLACK PIPE TRAIL

*Nawaimaka Str.*

CLIFF TRAIL

S
E — W
N

HALEMANU ROAD

TO HWY 50

P

HALEMANU-KOKEE TRAIL

KOKEE ROAD

# WAIPOO FALLS

ALSO SEE MAPS ON PAGES 14 • 19

# Hike 7
# Kukui Trail to overlooks

**Hiking distance:** 2 miles round trip
**Hiking time:** 1.5 hours
**Elevation gain:** 750 feet
**Maps:** U.S.G.S. Waimea Canyon
　　　　Earthwalk Press Northwestern Kauai Recreation Map

**Summary of hike:** This hike follows the first mile of the Kukui Trail into Waimea Canyon, descending to two spectacular viewpoints, each with a bench. Across the canyon are several waterfalls that stay in view throughout the one-mile descent. Waialae Falls is the dominant waterfall plunging off the cliffs. Wild goats are frequently visible along the canyon ridges.

**Driving directions:** From the junction of Waimea Canyon Drive and Kokee Road in Waimea Canyon (directions to junction on page 18) drive north 1.8 miles to the signed trailhead on the right between mile markers 8 and 9. Parking pullouts are on the west (left) side of the road, directly across from the trailhead.

From Kokee Lodge and museum, drive 6.9 miles down canyon (south) to the trailhead on the left.

**Hiking directions:** Follow the Iliau Nature Loop on the right. After 100 yards, the nature loop bears left (a 15-minute side trip). Take the signed right fork on the Kukui Trail past the covered picnic area. Switchbacks lead downhill a quarter mile into the canyon to the first viewing area, graced with a bench. Quarter-mile markers are placed along the trail. Every step takes you deeper into the canyon and offers a changing view and perspective. Continue down to a second viewing area on an eroded promontory with a bench, just beyond the one-mile marker. The second viewing area is the turnaround point for this hike.

To hike further, the trail continues to the canyon floor at the Waimea River and Wiliwili Camp (Hike 8).

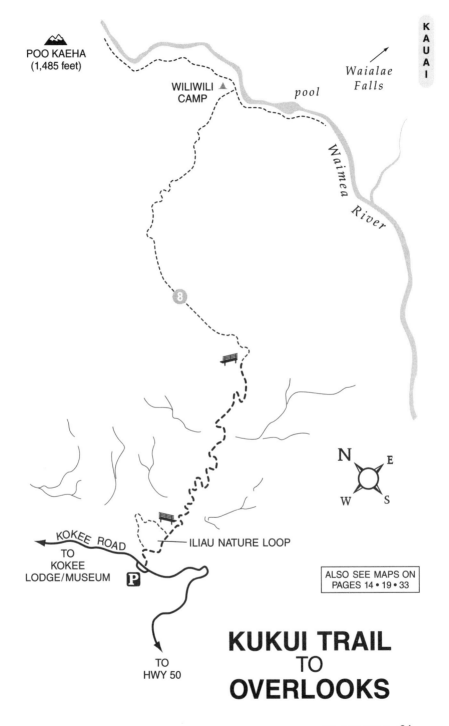

POO KAEHA
(1,485 feet)

WILIWILI
CAMP

pool

*Waialae*
*Falls*

K
A
U
A
I

*Waimea River*

8

N
E
W
S

KOKEE ROAD
TO
KOKEE
LODGE/MUSEUM

P

ILIAU NATURE LOOP

ALSO SEE MAPS ON
PAGES 14 • 19 • 33

TO
HWY 50

# KUKUI TRAIL
## TO
# OVERLOOKS

# Hike 8
# Kukui Trail to Waimea River

**Hiking distance:** 5 miles round trip
**Hiking time:** 3 hours
**Elevation gain:** 2,300 feet
**Maps:** U.S.G.S. Waimea Canyon
        Earthwalk Press Northwestern Kauai Recreation Map

**Summary of hike:** The Kukui Trail is the shortest route to the base of Waimea Canyon. The steep descent drops 2,300 feet to the canyon floor at the Waimea River, following a series of switchbacks on the west canyon wall. The canyon views along the path continually change due to cloud cover, changing light, elevation, and angles. The trail ends at Wiliwili Camp, a campsite with a covered shelter and table at the edge of the river.

**Driving directions:** From the junction of Waimea Canyon Drive and Kokee Road in Waimea Canyon (directions to junction on page 18) drive north 1.8 miles to the signed trailhead on the right between mile markers 8 and 9. Parking pullouts are on the west (left) side of the road, directly across from the trailhead.
    From Kokee Lodge and museum, drive 6.9 miles down canyon (south) to the trailhead on the left.

**Hiking directions:** Follow the Iliau Nature Loop on the right. After 100 yards, take the signed right fork on the Kukui Trail. Mileage markers are placed along the trail every quarter mile. Switchbacks lead steeply downhill along a ridge to a bench and viewing area at a quarter mile. Continue downhill to a second viewing area with a bench at one mile. Follow the ridgeline to a saddle. Bear left and head north down the bare hillside towards Poo Kaeha, the prominent formation to the north. Curve to the right, heading east into the forest. Zigzag downhill through the shady canopy, emerging at Wiliwili Camp and the Waimea River Trail. The river trail parallels the boulder-lined river in both directions. Downstream is a large pool. Return by climbing out of the canyon on the same trail.

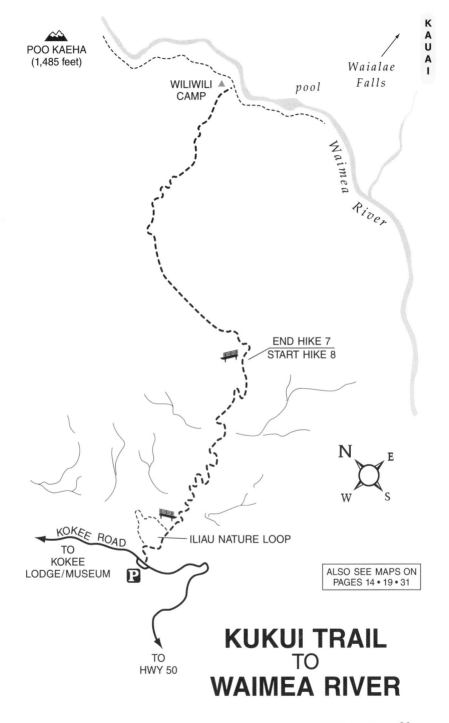

POO KAEHA
(1,485 feet)

K
A
U
A
I

Waialae
Falls

pool

Waimea River

WILIWILI
CAMP

END HIKE 7
START HIKE 8

N
E
W
S

ILIAU NATURE LOOP

KOKEE ROAD
TO
KOKEE
LODGE/MUSEUM

P

TO
HWY 50

ALSO SEE MAPS ON
PAGES 14 • 19 • 31

# KUKUI TRAIL
# TO
# WAIMEA RIVER

# Hike 9
# Shipwreck Beach
## KEONILOA BAY

**Hiking distance:** 2 miles round trip
**Hiking time:** 1 hour
**Elevation gain:** 50 feet
**Maps:** U.S.G.S. Koloa

**Summary of hike:** Shipwreck Beach, in Keoniloa Bay, is a half-mile crescent of sandy beach. The bay sits between the lava rocks of Kaneaukai and the lithified sand dune bluff of Makawehi Point. Trails crisscross the Makawehi cliffs, offering commanding views out to sea. Exploring the cliffs leads to beautifully sculpted rock formations, coves, caves, tidepools, and magnificent views up the rugged coastline and the Hoary Head Range.

**Driving directions:** From Lihue, drive 6.5 miles west on Highway 50 to Maluhia Road/Highway 520 between mile markers 6 and 7. Turn left and drive through the eucalyptus "Tree Tunnel." Head 3.3 miles to Koloa Road in the town of Koloa. Turn right and make a quick left onto Poipu Beach Road. Continue 3.6 miles to Ainako Street, just past the Hyatt Regency Kauai, and turn right. (Poipu Beach Road becomes Weliweli Road en route.) Go 0.2 miles to the public parking lot on the right at the beachfront.

**Hiking directions:** Walk down to the sand beach, and bear left towards the large Makawehi bluffs, jutting out into the ocean. Along the back side of the sandy beach, a forested path leads to the lithified sandstone cliffs. Several paths lead up to the promontory overlooking the ocean. A myriad of paths comb the formation through groves of twisted ironwood trees, vegetated sand dunes, and across the barren rock cliffs. Trails follow the cliff's edge and climb up to the sandy summit. Choose your own route and turnaround spot.

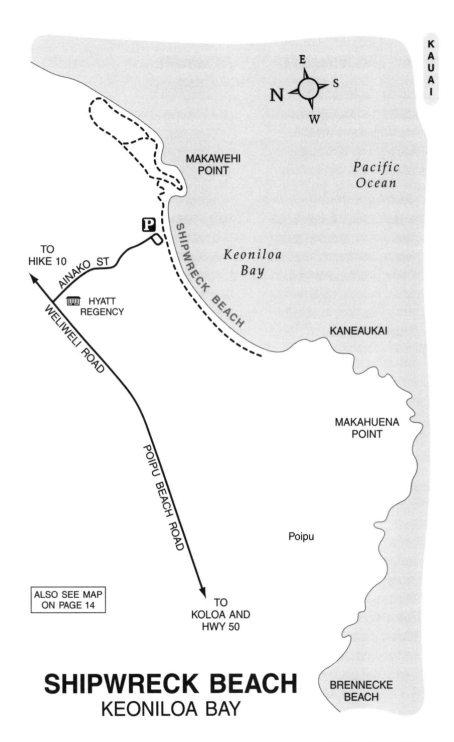

K A U A I

E
N ⊕ S
W

MAKAWEHI
POINT

*Pacific Ocean*

P

TO
HIKE 10

AINAKO ST

HYATT
REGENCY

WELIWELI ROAD

SHIPWRECK BEACH

*Keoniloa Bay*

KANEAUKAI

POIPU BEACH ROAD

MAKAHUENA
POINT

Poipu

ALSO SEE MAP
ON PAGE 14

TO
KOLOA AND
HWY 50

BRENNECKE
BEACH

# SHIPWRECK BEACH
## KENILOA BAY

# Hike 10
# Mahaulepu Beach to Kawelikoa Point

**Hiking distance:** 5 miles round trip
**Hiking time:** 2.5 hours
**Elevation gain:** 100 feet
**Maps:** U.S.G.S. Koloa and Lihue

**Summary of hike:** The trail from Mahaulepu Beach follows isolated 100-foot cliffs to Kawelikoa Point, passing weather-sculpted rock formations, sharp pinnacles, coves and caves, blowholes, natural bridges, and awesome coastal views. The views extend across the high mountain ridges of the Haupu (Hoary Head) Range and up the scalloped coastline.

**Driving directions:** From Lihue, drive 6.5 miles west on Highway 50 to Maluhia Road/Highway 520 between mile markers 6 and 7. Turn left and drive through the eucalyptus "Tree Tunnel." Head 3.3 miles to Koloa Road in the town of Koloa. Turn right and make a quick left onto Poipu Beach Road. Continue 5.3 miles (the pavement ends after 3.7 miles and becomes Weliweli Road) to a 4-way junction. Turn right and drive 0.4 miles to a T-junction. The beach access parking area is on the right.

**Hiking directions:** The well-defined path leads through a lush forest to the sandy, tree-lined beach. To the right, the steep cliffs of Punahoa Point extend out into the sea. At the base of the cliffs are tidepools. Paths lead up the cliffs to scenic overlooks. To the other side of Mahaulepu Beach, follow the shoreline between the ocean and the trees. Walk 0.3 miles northeast, crossing the dunes at Kamala Point into Kawailoa Bay. At the east end of the bay are sculpted lava formations. Paths cross the tree-covered cliffs to Haula Beach, a pocket beach between Paoo and Naakea Points. The wild beauty of the eroded cliffs and crashing surf is truly spectacular. The trail crosses the cliffs, reaching Kawelikoa Point at 2.5 miles. Return along the same path.

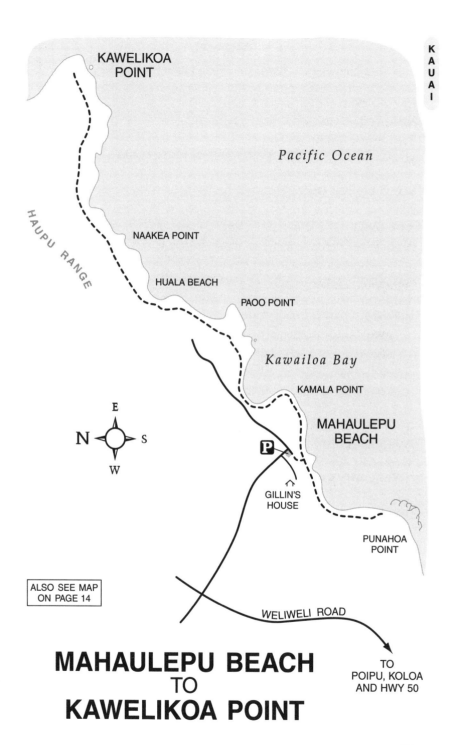

KAWELIKOA
POINT

K
A
U
A
I

*Pacific Ocean*

HAUPU RANGE

NAAKEA POINT

HUALA BEACH

PAOO POINT

*Kawailoa Bay*

KAMALA POINT

MAHAULEPU
BEACH

E
N—S
W

P

GILLIN'S
HOUSE

PUNAHOA
POINT

ALSO SEE MAP
ON PAGE 14

WELIWELI ROAD

TO
POIPU, KOLOA
AND HWY 50

# MAHAULEPU BEACH
TO
# KAWELIKOA POINT

# Hike 11
# Powerline Trail
## (SOUTHERN ACCESS)

**Hiking distance:** 5 miles round trip
**Hiking time:** 2.5 hours
**Elevation gain:** 800 feet
**Maps:** U.S.G.S. Waialeale
       Recreation Map of Eastern Kauai

**Summary of hike:** The Powerline Trail is a 10.5-mile trail that links the interior valleys with the north shore at Princeville. The trail, which follows powerlines, is a dirt road cut through the wilderness. The trail runs along the east side of Mount Waialeale, the wettest spot on earth. This hike from the southern trailhead follows the first 2.5 miles of the muddy trail to an overlook with views of two beautiful waterfalls. For a strenuous all-day event, this trail can be combined with Hike 25 for a fantastic one-way shuttle hike. (It is recommended to start from Hike 25 for the one-way hike.)

**Driving directions:** From Lihue, drive six miles north on Highway 56 to Kuamoo Road/Highway 580, the first intersection after crossing the Wailua River. Turn left and continue 6.9 miles to the Keahua Arboretum. There are parking lots on both sides of the road. You may park here and walk a quarter mile to the trailhead, or drive across the Keahua Stream and park on the right by the signed trailhead.

**Hiking directions:** Walk northwest past the arboretum on Highway 580. Wade across Keahua Stream to the signed trail on the right (north) side of the road at a quarter mile. Take the trail to the right and head up the rocky road. At the top of the first hill, a second access route joins the main trail. Stay to the right, dodging muddy pools on the vividly red clay road. To the west are views (weather permitting) of Kawaikini, the summit of Kauai at 5,243 feet, and Mount Waialeale. The jagged peaks of the Haupu (Hoary Head) Ridge can be seen to the southeast

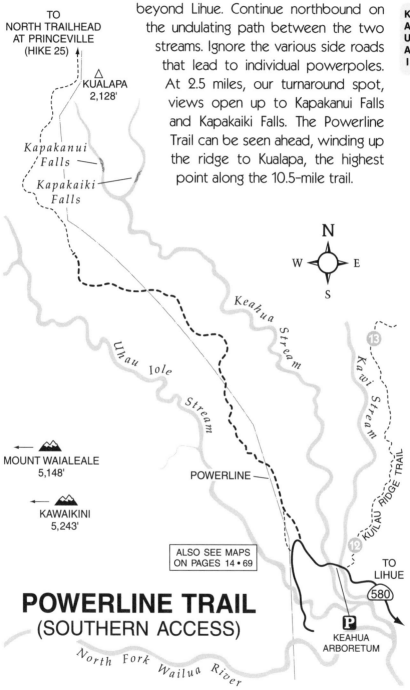

beyond Lihue. Continue northbound on the undulating path between the two streams. Ignore the various side roads that lead to individual powerpoles. At 2.5 miles, our turnaround spot, views open up to Kapakanui Falls and Kapakaiki Falls. The Powerline Trail can be seen ahead, winding up the ridge to Kualapa, the highest point along the 10.5-mile trail.

TO NORTH TRAILHEAD AT PRINCEVILLE (HIKE 25)

*Kapakanui Falls*

*Kapakaiki Falls*

K A U A I

N
W E
S

*Keahua Stream*

*Uhau Iole Stream*

*Kawi Stream*

MOUNT WAIALEALE 5,148'

KAWAIKINI 5,243'

POWERLINE

KUILAU RIDGE TRAIL

ALSO SEE MAPS ON PAGES 14 • 69

TO LIHUE

580

# POWERLINE TRAIL
## (SOUTHERN ACCESS)

P KEAHUA ARBORETUM

*North Fork Wailua River*

# Hike 12
# Kuilau Ridge Trail to overlook

**Hiking distance:** 2.4 miles round trip
**Hiking time:** 1.5 hours
**Elevation gain:** 400 feet
**Maps:** U.S.G.S. Waialeale and Kapaa
Recreational Map of Eastern Kauai

**Summary of hike:** This hike follows the first section of the forested Kuilau Ridge Trail (Hike 13), an old 4-wheel drive road. This path leads to a picnic shelter and overlook on a grassy plateau with impressive views. The panoramas extend west across the lush hillsides and beautiful valley to Mount Waialeale (weather permitting) and seaward to Nounou Mountain and Hoary Head.

**Driving directions:** From Lihue, drive six miles north on Highway 56 to Kuamoo Road/Highway 580, the first intersection after crossing the Wailua River. Turn left and continue 6.9 miles to the Keahua Arboretum. There are parking lots on both sides of the road.

**Hiking directions:** From the Keahua Arboretum, walk back along the road 100 yards to the signed trail on the left (north) side of the road. Bear left, leaving the valley, and ascend the ridge on the old road above Kawi Stream. Heading north, the trail skirts the ridge on the east. Stay on the main trail, passing various side paths. A large, flat grassy area with a sheltered picnic table is reached at 1.2 miles. From this resting spot, there are beautiful panoramic views of the many ridges and valleys. There are more stunning vistas within the next quarter mile. After relaxing and savoring the views, return along the same trail.

To hike further, the Kuilau Ridge Trail continues to a junction on a small knoll with the Moalepe Trail (Hikes 13 and 14).

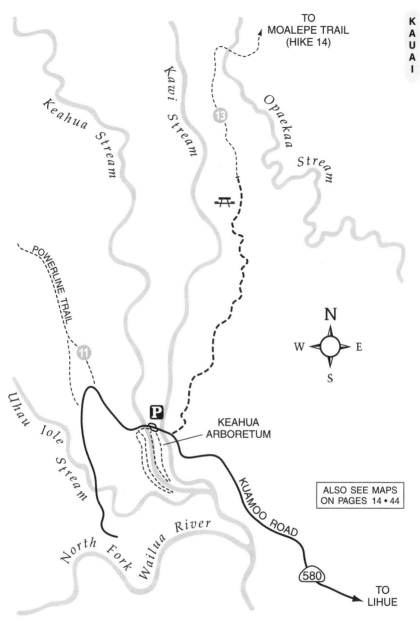

TO
MOALEPE TRAIL
(HIKE 14)

*Kawi Stream*

*Keahua Stream*

*Opaekaa Stream*

⑬

POWERLINE TRAIL

⑪

N
W    E
S

*Uhau Iole Stream*

**P**

KEAHUA
ARBORETUM

ALSO SEE MAPS
ON PAGES 14 • 44

KUAMOO ROAD

*North Fork Wailua River*

580

TO
LIHUE

# KUILAU RIDGE TRAIL
## TO
# OVERLOOK

# Hike 13
# Kuilau Ridge Trail to Moalepe Trail

**Hiking distance:** 4.4 miles round trip
**Hiking time:** 2.5 hours
**Elevation gain:** 700 feet
**Maps:** U.S.G.S. Waialeale and Kapaa
Recreational Map of Eastern Kauai

map
next page

**Summary of hike:** The Kuilau Ridge Trail begins at the Keahua Arboretum and climbs a forested ridge in the Lihue–Koloa Forest Reserve. Along the way, panoramic views open up across the rolling hillsides and picturesque valley to Mount Waialeale to the west, the Makaleha Mountains to the north, and the Pacific Ocean to the east. This trail can be combined with the Moalepe Trail (Hike 14) for a one-way, 4.6-mile shuttle hike.

**Driving directions:** From Lihue, drive 6 miles north on Highway 56 to Kuamoo Road/Highway 580, the first intersection after crossing the Wailua River. Turn left and continue 6.9 miles to the Keahua Arboretum. There are parking lots on both sides of the road.

**Hiking directions:** Follow the hiking directions for Hike 12 to the picnic shelter and overlook. From the picnic shelter, continue up the ridge. The winding path zigzags along a narrow ridge between Kawi Stream and Opaekaa Stream. To the east is a wonderful view of Nounou (Sleeping Giant) Mountain and the ocean at Kapaa. Cross a wooden footbridge over Opaekaa Stream, and climb up to the ridge in a clearing. Follow the Kamoohoopulu Ridge for 2.1 miles to the Moalepe Trail. The trail junction is on a small, flat grassy knoll by an old metal "End Kuilau Trail" sign. From the knoll are close-up views of the Makaleha Mountains. To the right is the Moalepe Trail (Hike 14).

# Hike 14
# Moalepe Trail to Kuilau Ridge Trail

**Hiking distance:** 5 miles round trip
**Hiking time:** 2.5 hours
**Elevation gain:** 700 feet
**Maps:** U.S.G.S. Kapaa
       Recreational Map of Eastern Kauai

**map
next page**

**Summary of hike:** The Moalepe Trail climbs up to the Kuilau Ridge in the foothills of the Makaleha Mountains. The first mile crosses pastureland on a red dirt road with panoramas of the lush jagged canyons and ridges of the Makaleha Mountains. Moalepe Stream winds its way down the valley on the north side of the trail. The trail ends at a junction with the Kuilau Ridge Trail (Hike 13) in the forest reserve. These two trails can be combined for a one-way, 4.6-mile shuttle hike.

**Driving directions:** From Lihue, drive six miles north on Highway 56 to Kuamoo Road/Highway 580, the first inter-section after crossing the Wailua River. Turn left and continue 2.8 miles to Kamalu Road/Highway 581. Turn right and drive 1.6 miles to Olohena Road. Turn left and go 1.6 miles to the end of the paved road at the intersection with Waipouli Road. Park in the pullout on the left by the signed Moalepe Trail.

**Hiking directions:** Hike northwest on the red dirt road, gently gaining elevation. The road is a right-of-way through private property to the forest reserve boundary. Cross the open country and pastureland to the end of the fenceline at 1.1 miles. Follow the muddy trail as it twists and curves up the nar-rowing mountain ridge towards Kuilau Ridge. At 2.5 miles, the trail ends on Kamoohoopulu Ridge at a small, flat grassy knoll above Moalepe Stream. From the knoll are close-up views of the Makaleha Mountains. A short distance to the left is an old metal "End Kuilau Trail" sign, our turnaround spot. This is where the Moalepe Trail connects with the Kuilau Ridge Trail from the south (Hike 13).

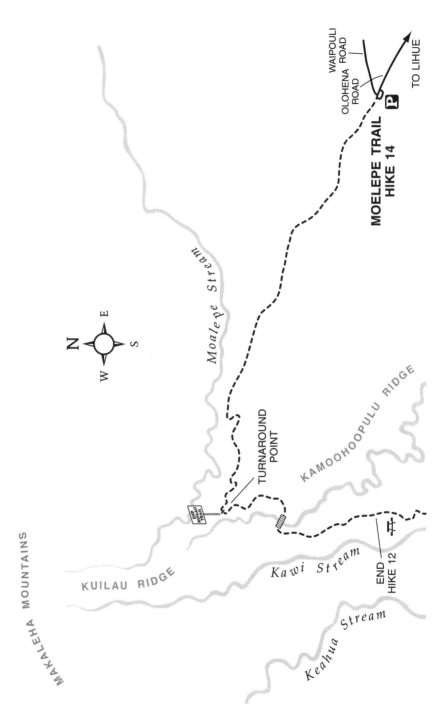

WAIPOULI ROAD
OLOHENA ROAD

P

TO LIHUE

MOELEPE TRAIL
HIKE 14

*Moalepe Stream*

N
E
S
W

KAMOOHOOPULU RIDGE

TURNAROUND
POINT

END
KUILAU
TRAIL

KUILAU RIDGE

*Kawi Stream*

END
HIKE 12

*Keahua Stream*

MAKALEHA MOUNTAINS

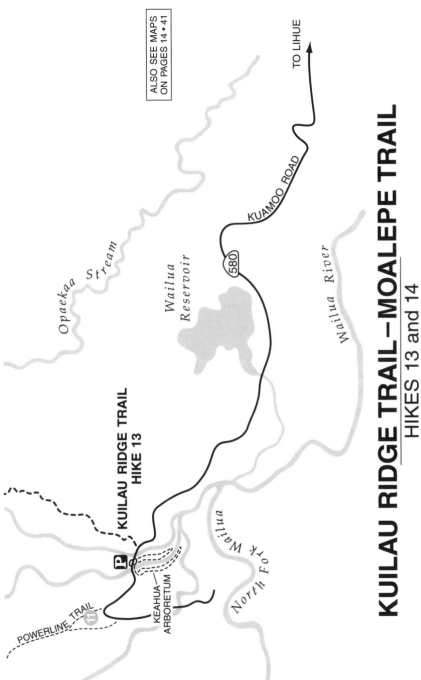

ALSO SEE MAPS
ON PAGES 14 • 41

TO LIHUE

KUAMOO ROAD

580

*Opaekaa Stream*

*Wailua Reservoir*

*Wailua River*

KUILAU RIDGE TRAIL
HIKE 13

P

KEAHUA
ARBORETUM

POWERLINE TRAIL

*North Fork Wailua*

KAUAI

# KUILAU RIDGE TRAIL–MOALEPE TRAIL
## HIKES 13 and 14

# Hike 15
# Nounou Mountain Trail West to Alii Vista Hale
## NOUNOU MOUNTAIN (SLEEPING GIANT)

**Hiking distance:** 3 miles round trip
**Hiking time:** 1.5 hours
**Elevation gain:** 800 feet
**Maps:** U.S.G.S. Kapaa
      Recreational Map of Eastern Kauai

**Summary of hike:** The Nounou Mountain Trail West is one of the three trails that climb to the summit of Nounou Mountain, known as Sleeping Giant. The hike begins on the west side of the mountain and climbs through the forest to Alii Vista Hale, a picnic shelter and overlook at the summit. The summit has great views of the Makaleha Mountains, Mount Waialeale, the Wailua River, the Coconut Coast, and the seacoast communities.

**Driving directions:** From Lihue, drive six miles north on Highway 56 to Kuamoo Road/Highway 580, the first intersection after crossing the Wailua River. Turn left and continue 2.8 miles to Kamalu Road/Highway 581. Turn right and drive 1.2 miles to the signed Nounou Mountain Trail West on the right (next to 1055 Kamalu Road) and park.

**Hiking directions:** Head east on the wide forest reserve right-of-way between rows of private homes and a cattle ranch. This public access trail reaches the forested footpath at the base of Nounou Mountain at 0.3 miles. Head uphill, weaving through a canopy of guava and oak trees to a signed junction in a distinct grove of Norfolk Island pines. The Kuamoo–Nounou Trail (Hike 17) is straight ahead. Curve left through a lane bordered by two parallel rows of Norfolk Island pines. Switchbacks lead up the steep trail along the contours of the mountain. At 1.4 miles, the West Trail ends at a junction with the East Trail (Hike 18). Take the right fork on the Nounou Mountain Trail East to Alii Vista Hale, a picnic shelter on a grassy knoll. After enjoying the panoramas, return along the same trail.

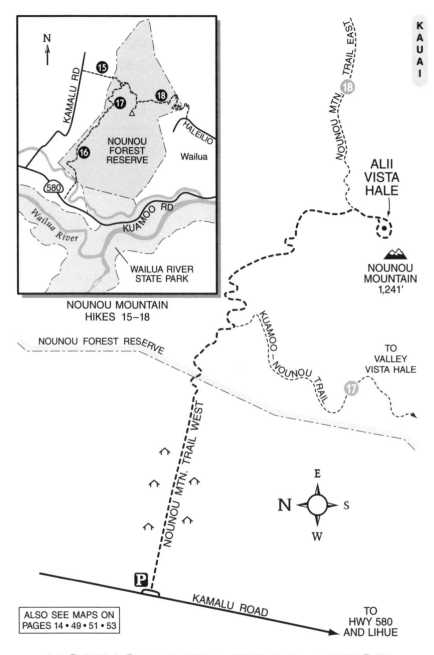

N

15

KAMALU RD

17

18

NOUNOU FOREST RESERVE

16

580

Wailua River

KUAMOO RD

HALEILIO

Wailua

WAILUA RIVER STATE PARK

NOUNOU MOUNTAIN HIKES 15–18

K
A
U
A
I

NOUNOU MTN. TRAIL EAST

18

ALII VISTA HALE

NOUNOU MOUNTAIN 1,241'

KUAMOO NOUNOU TRAIL

17

TO VALLEY VISTA HALE

NOUNOU FOREST RESERVE

NOUNOU MTN. TRAIL WEST

E
N — S
W

P

KAMALU ROAD

TO HWY 580 AND LIHUE

ALSO SEE MAPS ON PAGES 14 • 49 • 51 • 53

# NOUNOU MTN. TRAIL WEST
## TO ALII VISTA HALE

# Hike 16
# Kuamoo—Nounou Trail to Valley Vista Hale
## NOUNOU MOUNTAIN (SLEEPING GIANT)

**Hiking distance:** 1.5 miles round trip
**Hiking time:** 1 hour
**Elevation gain:** 150 feet
**Maps:** U.S.G.S. Kapaa
Recreational Map of Eastern Kauai

**Summary of hike:** This beautiful mountain path, which leads to panoramic views, follows the first portion of the Kuamoo—Nounou Trail for a short walk into the Nounou reserve. The hike begins on the valley floor by Opaekaa Stream, a half mile upstream from the waterfall. The trail crosses a footbridge over the stream and leads to Valley Vista Hale, a grassy vista point with a sheltered picnic table perched on the side of the mountain. From the overlook are views of the Kalepa Ridge across the Wailua River, Lihue Basin, and the Makaleha Mountains.

**Driving directions:** From Lihue, drive six miles north on Highway 56 to Kuamoo Road/Highway 580, the first intersection after crossing the Wailua River. Turn left and continue 2.4 miles to the parking area on the right. The parking area is 0.7 miles past Opaekaa Falls, directly across from Nelia Street.

**Hiking directions:** From the parking area, a sign on the fence marks the trailhead. Follow the tree-lined lane 0.2 miles to the footbridge over Opaekaa Stream. After crossing, the trail curves left along a fenceline, then winds its way up the side of Nounou Mountain into a dense forest canopy. A short distance ahead, the trail breaks out of the forest to views of the Lihue Basin. At 0.75 miles you will be treated to Valley Vista Hale, a picnic shelter and overlook. This is the turnaround point. After resting and savoring the views, return along the same trail.

To hike further, the Kuamoo-Nounou Trail continues another mile up the mountain to a junction with the Nounou Mountain Trail West (Hike 15).

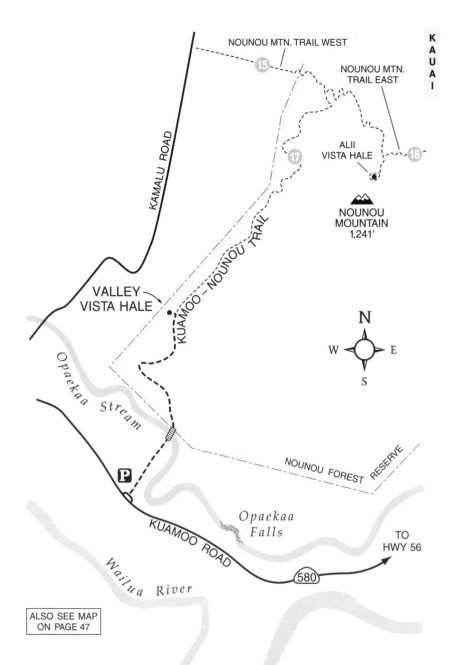

# KUAMOO–NOUNOU TRAIL
## TO VALLEY VISTA HALE

ALSO SEE MAP ON PAGE 47

# Hike 17
# Kuamoo—Nounou Trail to
# Nounou Mountain Trail West
## NOUNOU MOUNTAIN (SLEEPING GIANT)

**Hiking distance:** 3.6 miles round trip
**Hiking time:** 2 hours
**Elevation gain:** 400 feet
**Maps:** U.S.G.S. Kapaa
　　　　　Recreational Map of Eastern Kauai

**Summary of hike:** The Kuamoo—Nounou Trail is one of three access trails leading up to the summit of Nounou Mountain, known as the Sleeping Giant. This route follows the southern access through the forest reserve along a cliffside shelf on the west side of the mountain. The forested trail offers picturesque views of Mount Waialeale, Kawaikini, and the Makaleha Mountains.

**Driving directions:** From Lihue, drive six miles north on Highway 56 to Kuamoo Road/Highway 580, the first intersection after crossing the Wailua River. Turn left and continue 2.4 miles to the parking area on the right. The parking area is 0.7 miles past Opaekaa Falls, directly across from Nelia Street.

**Hiking directions:** Follow the hiking directions of Hike 16 to Valley Vista Hale, the picnic shelter and overlook. From the shelter, hike northeast, contouring along the west flank of Nounou Mountain under the dense forest canopy. The path parallels the forest reserve boundary with frequent dips and rises, passing groves of guava, eucalyptus, and Norfolk Island pines. Near the end of the trail, gently descend to a junction with the Nounou Mountain Trail West at 1.8 miles. This is the resting and turnaround point for this hike. Return on the same trail.

To hike further, the Nounou Mountain Trail West (Hike 15) continues to the right through a lane bordered by two parallel rows of Norfolk Island pines. The trail climbs 1.5 miles up to Alii Vista Hale at the summit.

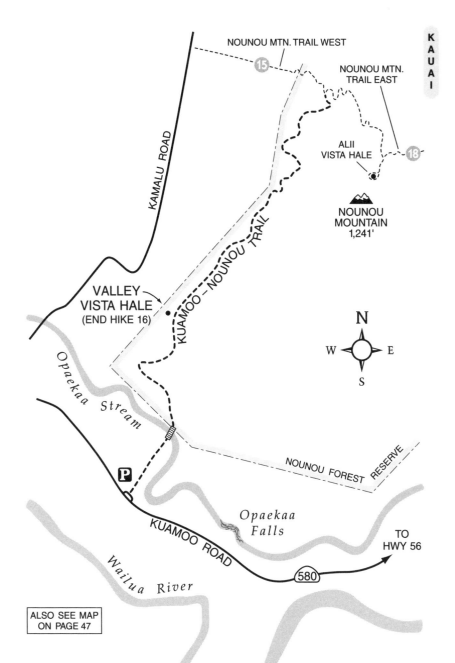

# KUAMOO–NOUNOU TRAIL
## TO NOUNOU MTN. TRAIL WEST

# Hike 18
# Nounou Mountain Trail East to Alii Vista Hale
## NOUNOU MOUNTAIN (SLEEPING GIANT)

**Hiking distance:** 3.5 miles round trip
**Hiking time:** 2 hours
**Elevation gain:** 1,000 feet
**Maps:** U.S.G.S. Kapaa
Recreational Map of Eastern Kauai

**Summary of hike:** The Nounou Mountain Trail East is one of the three trails that climbs up to the summit of Nounou Mountain, also known as Sleeping Giant. The trail follows the eastern access up a series of switchbacks through the forest. The path ends at Alii Vista Hale, a picnic shelter at the summit on the chest of the giant. Along the way are spectacular views of the Wailua River and the seacoast communities from Anahola to Lihue. From Alii Vista Hale are views to the west of the cloud-engulfed Mount Waialeale in the Makaleha Mountains, the headwaters for all seven major rivers on Kauai.

**Driving directions:** From Lihue, drive 6 miles north on Highway 56 to Haleilio Road, the second intersection after crossing the Wailua River. Turn left and continue 1.1 miles to the Nounou Mountain East trailhead parking lot on the right.

**Hiking directions:** The trail begins on the right side of the parking lot to the right of the rock wall. The path immediately enters the lush forest. Switchbacks allow for a gradual and easy ascent. At 0.7 miles, the path descends for a short distance, then regains the climb, passing numerous overlooks. The path crosses over to the west side of the ridge and back to the east a couple of times as it nears the top. Views alternate between the mountainous interior and the eastern coastline. The trail reaches a 3-way junction at 1.7 miles. The Nounou Mountain Trail West (Hike 15) bears to the right. Take the left fork a short distance to Alii Vista Hale, a picnic shelter on a flat, grassy knoll. After enjoying the summit, return along the same path.

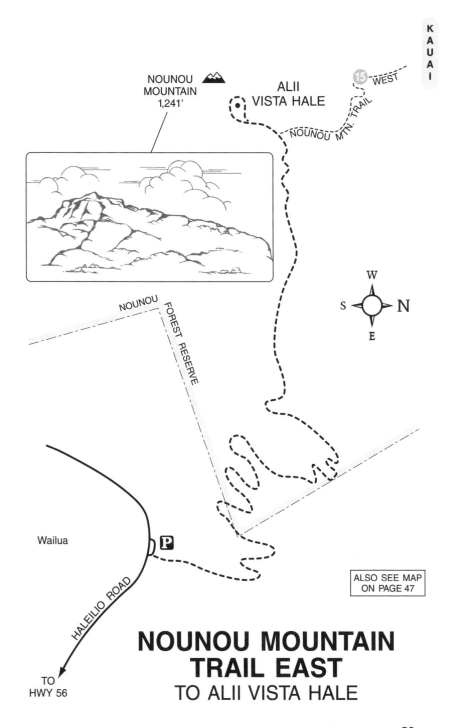

NOUNOU
MOUNTAIN
1,241'

ALII
VISTA HALE

KAUAI

15 WEST

NOUNOU MTN. TRAIL

NOUNOU

FOREST RESERVE

W
S — N
E

Wailua

P

ALSO SEE MAP
ON PAGE 47

HALEILIO ROAD

TO
HWY 56

# NOUNOU MOUNTAIN
# TRAIL EAST
## TO ALII VISTA HALE

# Hike 19
# North Kapaa Ocean Walk
# to Kealia Lookout

**Hiking distance:** 2 miles round trip
**Hiking time:** 1 hour
**Elevation gain:** 50 feet
**Maps:** U.S.G.S. Kapaa
             Recreation Map of Eastern Kauai

**Summary of hike:** This hike takes you along an old abandoned road perched above the ocean. The road, well hidden from the highway, was an old cane hauling route. The views along this rugged coastline are magnificent. A side trail leads up to Kealia Lookout, a grassy knoll and overlook with panoramic views up and down the jagged coastline.

**Driving directions:** From Lihue, drive 9 miles north on Highway 56 to the north end of Kapaa. Park in the pullout on the right (ocean) side of the road by mile marker 9. The pullout is across the road from Kapaa Jodo Mission at Hauaala Road.

**Hiking directions:** From the parking pullout, walk south 50 feet to the old road. Head northeast, following the ridge above the ocean. Along the way, various side paths lead down to the sandy beach. Near the far end of the road, at 0.8 miles, is a large knoll—Kealia Lookout. To the right, paths lead down to the ocean and up to the top of the knoll. From the summit are coastal views from Kealia Beach and Paliku Point in the north to Kapaa Beach in the south. At one mile, the trail rejoins Highway 56 by the Kapaa Stream bridge adjacent to Kealia Beach. Return to your car along the same path.

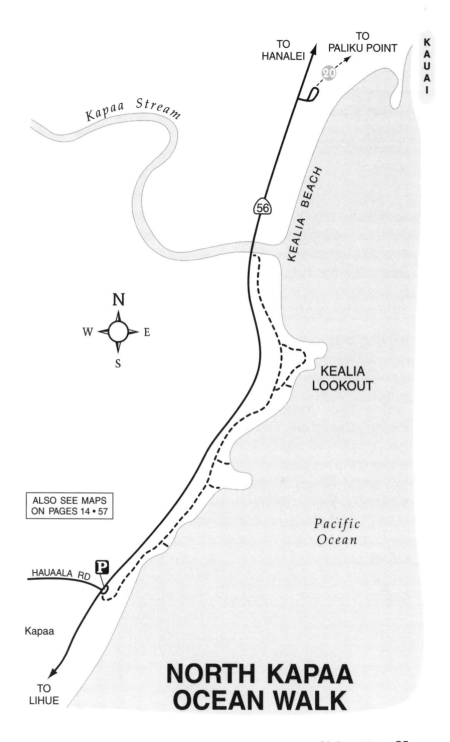

TO
HANALEI

TO
PALIKU POINT

K A U A I

20

*Kapaa Stream*

56

KEALIA BEACH

N
W   E
S

KEALIA
LOOKOUT

ALSO SEE MAPS
ON PAGES 14 • 57

*Pacific
Ocean*

HAUAALA RD

P

Kapaa

TO
LIHUE

# NORTH KAPAA
# OCEAN WALK

# Hike 20
# Kealia Cliffside Trail

**Hiking distance:** 2.4 miles round trip
**Hiking time:** 1.5 hours
**Elevation gain:** 50 feet
**Maps:** U.S.G.S. Kapaa

**Summary of hike:** Kealia Beach is a popular surfing beach bordered by rocky points. Kapaa Stream flows across the south end of the beach. At the north end is a sheltered cove protected by a jetty. The cliffside trail is an old cane hauling road that begins at the north end of this beach near the shorebreak. The graded, red dirt road overlooks the sea while following the edge of the cliffs to Paliku Point. From the point are dramatic coastal views.

**Driving directions:** From Lihue, drive 10.5 miles north on Highway 56 to the parking lot at the north end of Kealia Beach between mile markers 10 and 11. Turn right and park.

**Hiking directions:** Rather than following the shoreline, take the rock-lined road at the north end of the parking lot above the sandy beach. Head north towards the cliffs, parallel to the ocean. The path is perched on the hillside above the tidepools and crashing waves. At one mile, as you round the first point, is a trail split. Stay to the right, following close to the ocean. A short distance ahead, large boulders have been placed across the path where there was once a bridge. Take the footpath on the left across the ravine. The path returns back to the main trail on the red dirt road. To the right, a short detour leads to huge rock formations at the ocean bluffs and an old concrete platform jutting out to sea, once used as a pineapple loading pier. Return to the trail and continue north, reaching Paliku Point at 1.2 miles. Leave the road and explore the point and the magnificent views. To return, retrace your steps.

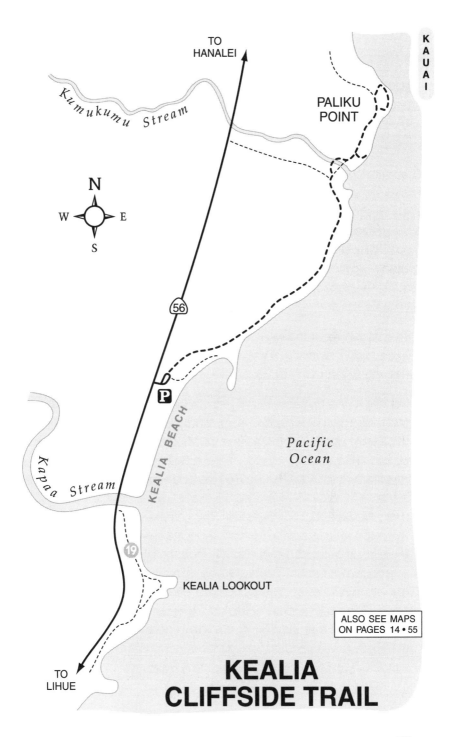

TO
HANALEI

K
A
U
A
I

*Kumukumu Stream*

PALIKU
POINT

N
W    E
S

56

P

KEALIA BEACH

*Kapaa Stream*

19

*Pacific
Ocean*

KEALIA LOOKOUT

ALSO SEE MAPS
ON PAGES 14 • 55

TO
LIHUE

# KEALIA
# CLIFFSIDE TRAIL

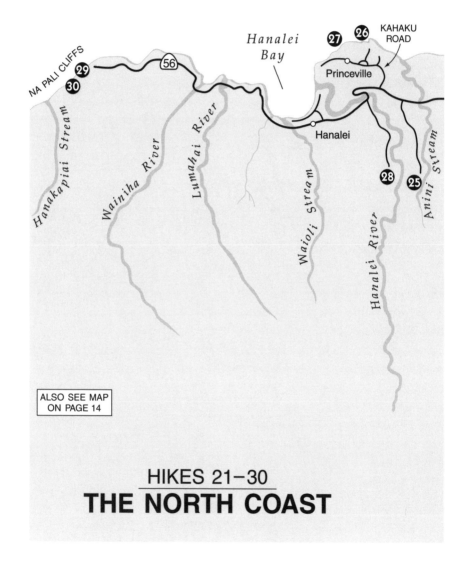

Pacific Ocean

Hanalei Bay

KAHAKU ROAD

NA PALI CLIFFS

㉙ ㉚

56

㉗ ㉖

Princeville

Hanalei

Hanakapiai Stream

Wainiha River

Lumahai River

Waioli Stream

Hanalei River

Anini Stream

㉘ ㉕

ALSO SEE MAP
ON PAGE 14

HIKES 21–30
# THE NORTH COAST

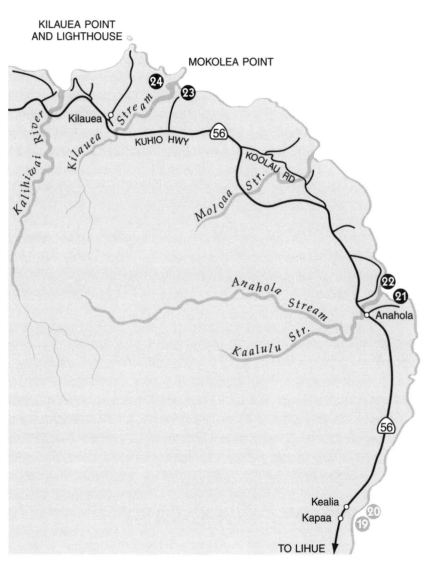

N
W   E
S

KILAUEA POINT
AND LIGHTHOUSE

MOKOLEA POINT

24

23

Kilauea

*Kilauea Stream*

*Kalihiwai River*

KUHIO HWY

56

KOOLAU RD

*Moloaa Str.*

*Anahola Stream*

22

21

Anahola

*Kaalulu Str.*

56

Kealia

Kapaa

20

19

TO LIHUE

# Hike 21
# Anahola Beach
## KAHALA POINT TO ANAHOLA STREAM

**Hiking distance:** 1.2 miles round trip
**Hiking time:** 1 hour
**Elevation gain:** Level
**Maps:** U.S.G.S. Anahola
       Recreation Map of Eastern Kauai

**Summary of hike:** Anahola Beach is a long, wide sandy beach on the south side of Anahola Bay. The bay, bordered by Kahala Point and Kuaehu Point, lies in a protected cove with a large offshore reef. Anahola Stream flows down from the inland mountains and divides the bay, separating Anahola Beach from Aliomanu Beach (Hike 22). Along the stream are large shallow pools. This beachside path travels through Anahola Beach County Park, a neighborhood park with a flat, grassy camping area in a shady ironwood and hau tree grove. The park has showers, restrooms, picnic tables, and barbecues.

**Driving directions:** From Lihue, drive 13.5 miles north on Highway 56 to Anahola Road between mile markers 13 and 14. Turn right and drive 0.8 miles to a parking lot at the east end of the bay. Turn left and park.

**Hiking directions:** Walk out to the oceanfront by the old cement pier pilings. Head east (right), following the sandy shoreline or the grassy, tree-lined path towards Kahala Point at the east end of the bay. The path ends near black lava rocks at the base of the bluffs. Heading back west, stroll along the shoreline to the mouth of Anahola Stream and a lagoon. When the stream is low, wade across to Aliomanu Beach (Hike 22), and continue north to Kuaehu Point. Return the way you came.

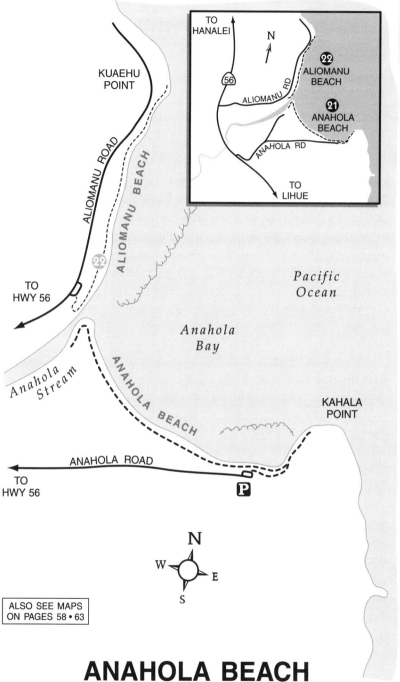

# ANAHOLA BEACH

# Hike 22
# Aliomanu Beach

**Hiking distance:** 1.2 miles round trip
**Hiking time:** 1 hour
**Elevation gain:** Level
**Maps:** U.S.G.S. Anahola
Recreation Map of Eastern Kauai

**Summary of hike:** This hike is an easy, meandering beach stroll on a narrow, tree-lined ribbon of sand along Anahola Bay. The half-mile stretch is bordered to the north by Kuaehu Point and to the south by Anahola Stream and a lagoon. Near the stream is a picnic area with tables in a shady grove of ironwood and kamani trees. The beach has an extensive offshore reef and is a popular fishing spot for locals. The views extend across Anahola Beach (Hike 21) to Kahala Point at the east tip of the bay. This walk may be combined with Hike 21 when Anahola Stream is low.

**Driving directions:** From Lihue, drive 14 miles north on Highway 56 to Aliomanu Road, just beyond mile marker 14. Turn right and drive 0.6 miles to the parking area at the south end of the beach, adjacent to Anahola Stream. Park on the right under the grove of ironwood trees.

**Hiking directions:** Walk through the shady picnic area along Anahola Stream and the lagoon. From the mouth of the stream, follow the sandy shoreline north, passing several beachside houses. At 0.6 miles, the strand reaches Kuaehu Point by a pile of black boulders at the north tip of the bay. This is our turn-around spot.

When the stream is low, wade across Anahola Stream to Anahola Beach. You may continue your hike to Kahala Point (Hike 21).

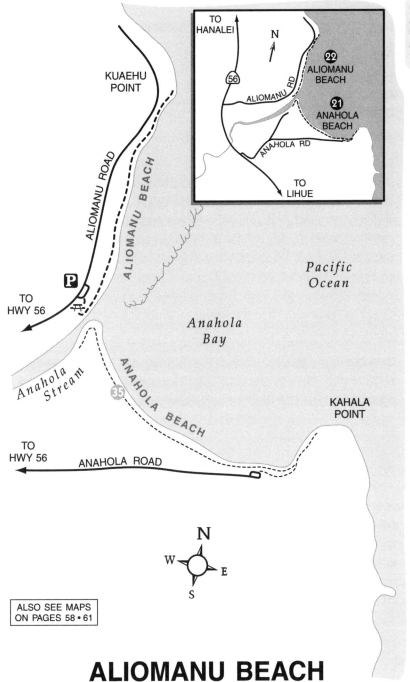

KAUAI

TO HANALEI

N

22 ALIOMANU BEACH

21 ANAHOLA BEACH

56

ALIOMANU RD

ANAHOLA RD

TO LIHUE

KUAEHU POINT

ALIOMANU ROAD

ALIOMANU BEACH

P

TO HWY 56

Pacific Ocean

Anahola Bay

Anahola Stream

35

ANAHOLA BEACH

KAHALA POINT

TO HWY 56

ANAHOLA ROAD

N
W E
S

ALSO SEE MAPS ON PAGES 58 • 61

# ALIOMANU BEACH

# Hike 23
# Kilauea Bay

**Hiking distance:** 1.2 miles round trip
**Hiking time:** 1 hour
**Elevation gain:** 100 feet
**Maps:** U.S.G.S. Anahola

**Summary of hike:** Kilauea Bay is a picturesque half-moon bay between two tree-covered rocky bluffs. Kahili Quarry Beach sits in this secluded cove fringed with groves of ironwood trees. Windswept cliffs line the east side of the bay. At the base of the cliffs are tidepools in the pile of lava rocks. Kilauea Stream and a lagoon border the western edge of the beach. Just past the mouth of the stream, the rock formations of Mokolea Point extend out to sea. The peninsula is part of the 160-acre Kilauea National Wildlife Refuge.

**Driving directions:** From Lihue, drive 21.5 miles north and west on Highway 56 to Wailapa Road between mile markers 21 and 22. Turn right and drive a half mile to an unpaved road on the left. Turn left and descend 0.6 miles, overlooking the Kilauea Stream, to an unimproved parking area at the end of the road.

**Hiking directions:** To the right, a short red dirt path leads through the forest to a grassy knoll overlooking the bay. To the left, take the two-track trail parallel to the bay through the lush forest. Several side paths lead down to the beach on the right. The main path winds through ironwood groves to Kilauea Stream and the lagoon at the mouth of the river. After enjoying this area, return along the beach. At the east end of the bay, the sand terminates at the cliffs by lava rocks and tidepools.

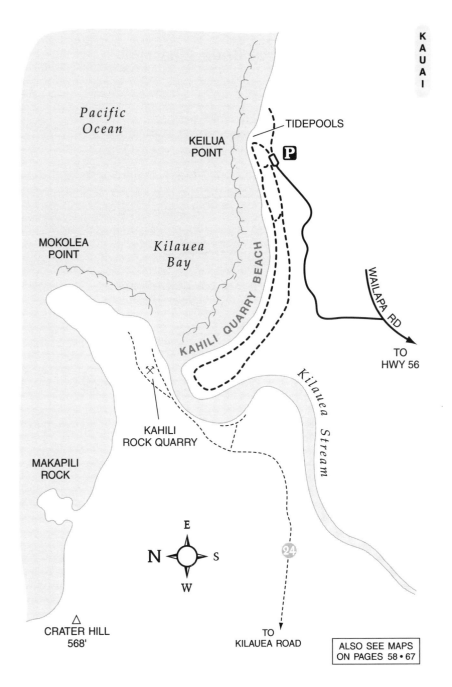

*Pacific
Ocean*

TIDEPOOLS

KEILUA
POINT

P

MOKOLEA
POINT

*Kilauea
Bay*

KAHILI QUARRY BEACH

WAILAPA RD

TO
HWY 56

*Kilauea
Stream*

KAHILI
ROCK QUARRY

MAKAPILI
ROCK

E

N S

W

△
CRATER HILL
568'

24

TO
KILAUEA ROAD

ALSO SEE MAPS
ON PAGES 58 • 67

# KILAUEA BAY

# Hike 24
# Kahili Rock Quarry

**Hiking distance:** 3 miles round trip
**Hiking time:** 1.5 hours
**Elevation gain:** 300 feet
**Maps:** U.S.G.S. Anahola

**Summary of hike:** Kahili Rock Quarry sits along the rugged cliffs of Mokolea Point, part of the Kilauea National Wildlife Refuge. The abandoned rock quarry overlooks the crescent-shaped Kilauea Bay from above Kilauea Stream and the blue Pacific. The views extend across the bay, which is rimmed by groves of ironwood trees, to the forested windswept cliffs along the bay's eastern edge. The hike follows an old rutted road to the ocean to the quarry and an overlook.

For a side trip, drive to the end of Kilauea Road to the Kilauea Lighthouse and national wildlife refuge at the end of the road.

**Driving directions:** From Lihue, drive 23.5 miles north on Highway 56 to the town of Kilauea. Turn right on Kolo Road, located between mile markers 23 and 24. Drive one block and turn left on Kilauea Road. Continue 0.7 miles through town to a dirt road on the right. Park along the right side of the road by the metal gate.

**Hiking directions:** Follow the unpaved road east along a row of mature ironwood trees teeming with the sounds of birds. At a half mile, the road begins a gradual descent past a banana orchard on the left. Kilauea Stream can be seen down in the river valley to the right. As the path curves left, views open up to the ocean and the lagoon at the mouth of the stream in Kilauea Bay. Near the bay is a trail fork. The right fork leads down to a flat grassy grove at the edge of the stream. The sandy cove across the stream is fringed with groves of iron-wood trees. The main trail continues straight, following the west edge of the bay towards Mokolea Point. Climb up the rocky road by the old quarry to a scenic overlook. Views extend across the bay to Keilua Point and Kepuhi Point farther east. Access is not allowed to Mokolea Point.

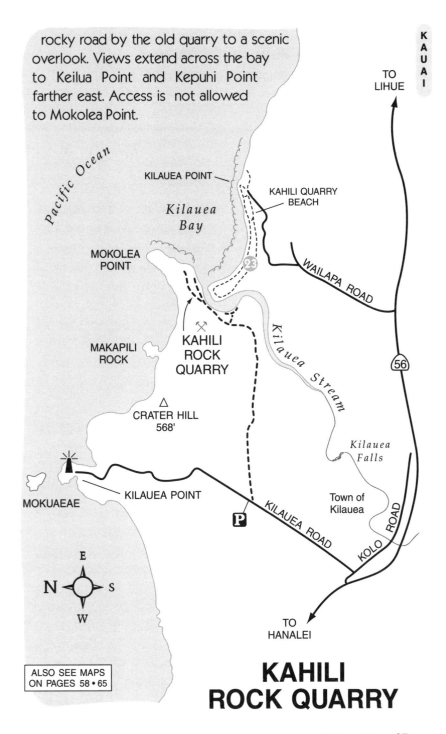

ALSO SEE MAPS
ON PAGES 58 • 65

# KAHILI
# ROCK QUARRY

# Hike 25
# Powerline Trail
## (NORTHERN ACCESS)

**Hiking distance:** 2.5 miles round trip
**Hiking time:** 1 hour
**Elevation gain:** 200 feet
**Maps:** U.S.G.S. Hanalei
Recreation Map of Eastern Kauai

**Summary of hike:** The Powerline Trail is a 10.5-mile trail through the interior mountain valleys, linking the north shore with the east side of the island. The trail is a red dirt road that follows powerlines through the forest reserve. This short hike starts at the trail's northern access and follows the first mile of the muddy dirt road. The trail travels above the Hanalei Valley, overlooking the river, Hanalei National Wildlife Refuge, and the ocean beyond Hanalei Bay. Through openings in the lush foliage, waterfalls can be seen falling off faraway cliffs. For a strenuous all-day experience, this trail can be combined with Hike 11 (the southern access route) for a fantastic one-way shuttle hike.

**Driving directions:** From Lihue, drive 27 miles north and west on Highway 56 to Pooku Road, located after mile marker 27. The turnoff is about a mile past the Princeville Airport by the horse stables. Turn left (south) and drive 1.9 miles to the trailhead parking area on the left, past the water tank by the hunters' check-in box. The last 0.2 miles are unpaved.

**Hiking directions:** Walk south on the red clay road lined with lush tropical vegetation. A side trail merges from the right at 0.2 miles. Continue gently uphill on several small dips and rises. At a half mile, views open up to the Hanalei National Wildlife Refuge and the Hanalei River on the right (west). As you approach the one-mile mark, which lies across the valley from the triangular-shaped peak of Hihimanu, watch for openings in the dense foliage. The views across the agricultural valley include numerous waterfalls dropping hundreds of feet off the

sheer cliffs of the mountains. This is our turnaround spot.
To hike further, the next few miles follow a gentle
grade with numerous ups and downs,
skirting the west flank of
Kapaka above the
Kalihiwai River.

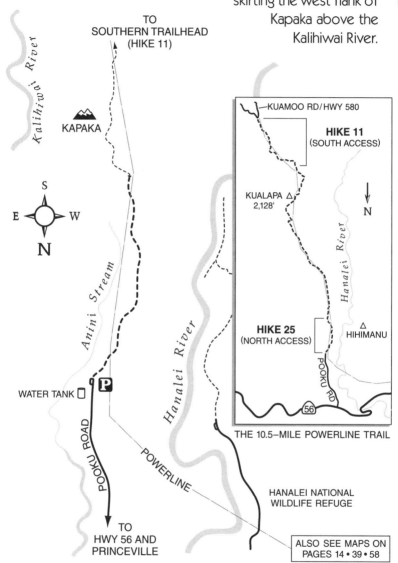

THE 10.5–MILE POWERLINE TRAIL

HANALEI NATIONAL
WILDLIFE REFUGE

ALSO SEE MAPS ON
PAGES 14 • 39 • 58

# POWERLINE TRAIL
## NORTHERN ACCESS

# Hike 26
# Sea Lodge Beach
## (KAWEONUI BEACH)

**Hiking distance:** 1 mile round trip
**Hiking time:** 1 hour
**Elevation gain:** 150 feet
**Maps:** U.S.G.S. Hanalei

**Summary of hike:** Sea Lodge Beach is a secluded beach at the base of the steep sea cliffs in Princeville. The small, protected cove is tucked into an indentation at the base of steep green cliffs. The trail winds through a tropical jungle to the sea at Kaweonui Point.

**Driving directions:** From Lihue, drive 28 miles north and west on Highway 56 to Kahaku Road at the Princeville sign, just before the Princeville Shopping Center. Turn right and drive 0.9 miles to Pepelani Road. Turn right and go 0.2 miles to Kaweonui Road. Turn right again and drive 0.4 miles to Keoniana Road. Turn right and park along the side of the road. (See inset map on page 73.)

**Hiking directions:** Walk 30 yards down Keoniana Road to a long paved driveway on the right. Bear right and head east past the gate on the service road. Walk downhill through the forest, and cross over a seasonal stream to the end of the road at a fenced pump installation. Take the left fork on the footpath along the right side of the stream to a trail split. The right fork leads to an overlook on the bluffs behind the Sea Cliff Hotel. Take the left fork down a few steps and across the stream. The jungle path winds downhill through lush vegetation. The trail is wet and precarious, demanding full concentration. Continue down a long series of gravel steps to the coast at Kaweonui Point. Curve left and watch for a short detour on the right to a lookout on Kaweonui Point, a black lava rock shelf. On the main trail continue west, curving into Sea Lodge Beach. The small pocket of sand is nestled at the base of the 150-foot cliffs.

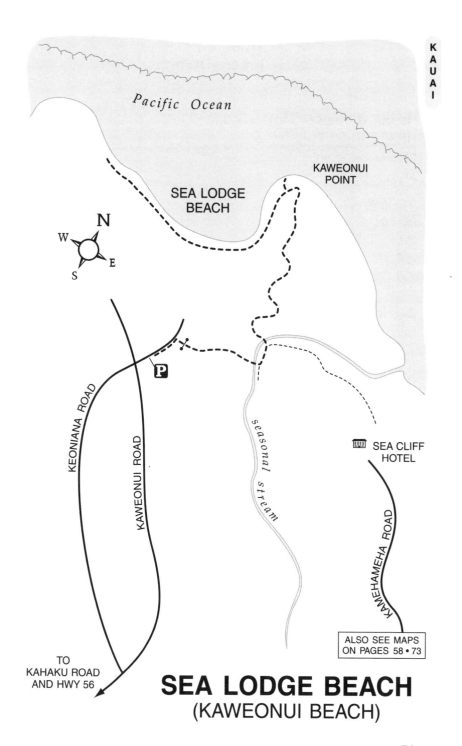

# SEA LODGE BEACH
## (KAWEONUI BEACH)

# Hike 27
# Queen's Bath

**Hiking distance:** 0.6 miles round trip
**Hiking time:** 30 minutes
**Elevation gain:** 150 feet
**Maps:** U.S.G.S. Hanalei

**Summary of hike:** Queen's Bath is a natural pool carved into the lava shelf at the base of the cliffs in Princeville. An inlet connects the pool to the ocean. Queen's Bath constantly changes due to the time of year, surf, and tides. During the winter, the bath may not be easy to identify due to the pounding surf. From the lava shelf and pool are beautiful mountain and coastal views. The trail parallels a stream past a freshwater waterfall and pool. There are steep inclines, loose footing, and narrow ledges. Use caution and good judgement while negotiating this path.

**Driving directions:** From Lihue, drive 28 miles north and west on Highway 56 to Kahaku Road at the Princeville sign, just before the Princeville Shopping Center. Turn right and drive 1.4 miles to Punahele Road and turn right. Continue 0.3 miles to the second Kapiolani Road intersection and turn right. Park in the signed parking lot on the left. (See inset map.)

**Hiking directions:** Take the well-defined path, past the caution signs, on the right side of the parking lot. Descend into the lush, shady forest. Tree roots on the trail are helpful for better footholds. Along the way, the path begins paralleling a stream on the right to the top of a waterfall and pool. Descend a short distance to a spur trail on the right leading to the pool at the base of the falls. Return to the main trail and continue downhill, following the stream towards the ocean. The path emerges from the forest to a large lava shelf at the sea. On the right, a waterfall cascades off the rocks into the ocean. Follow the lava rock shelf to the left, reaching Queen's Bath and the ocean inlet.

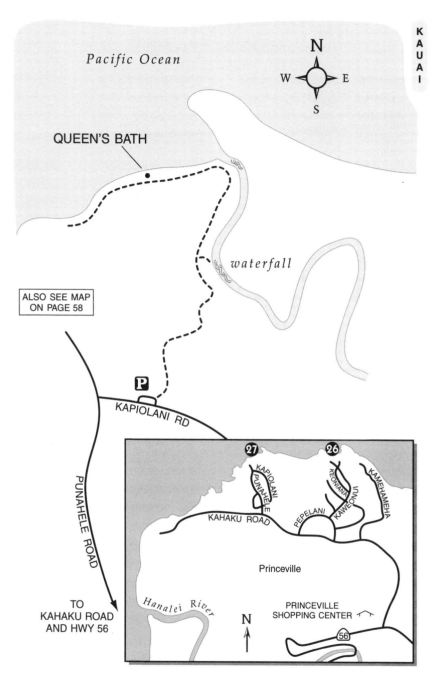

Pacific Ocean

QUEEN'S BATH

N
W • E
S

KAUAI

waterfall

ALSO SEE MAP
ON PAGE 58

P

KAPIOLANI RD

PUNAHELE ROAD

TO
KAHAKU ROAD
AND HWY 56

27

26

KAPIOLANI
PUNAHELE

KEONIANA
KAWEONUI
KAMEHAMEHA

PEPELANI

KAHAKU ROAD

Princeville

Hanalei River

N

PRINCEVILLE
SHOPPING CENTER

56

# QUEEN'S BATH

# Hike 28
# Hanalei River Trail
Recommended: mosquito repellent

**Hiking distance:** 3 miles round trip
**Hiking time:** 1.5 hours
**Elevation gain:** 200 feet
**Maps:** U.S.G.S. Hanalei
Northwestern Kauai Recreational Map

**Summary of hike:** This hike is a deep jungle experience in the Hanalei Valley. The trail takes you through tall bamboo forests, across streams, and into deep, dense tropical vegetation with overhanging branches, roots, and ferns. It leads to the Hanalei River, Kauai's largest river. White shoes are not recommended.

**Driving directions:** From Lihue, drive 30.5 miles north and west on Highway 56 towards Hanalei. Continue past Princeville. Just after crossing a long one-lane bridge over the Hanalei River, turn left on Ohiki Road. The sign at this turn reads "Hanalei National Wildlife Refuge." There are large cultivated taro fields on the right side of the road after the turn. Continue for two miles on this road, and park near the hunters' check-in booth.

**Hiking directions:** From the parking area, hike south along the rutted, muddy road through the tropical forest. At one mile the road narrows to a footpath. Watch on the left for a clearly visible trail that descends through a dense forest to the first stream crossing. Rocks can be used as stepping stones to ford the stream. Continue through the bamboo forest to a second stream crossing. A short distance after crossing, the path reaches the banks of the Hanalei River. Stroll upstream along the grassy banks of the river. Return along the same path.

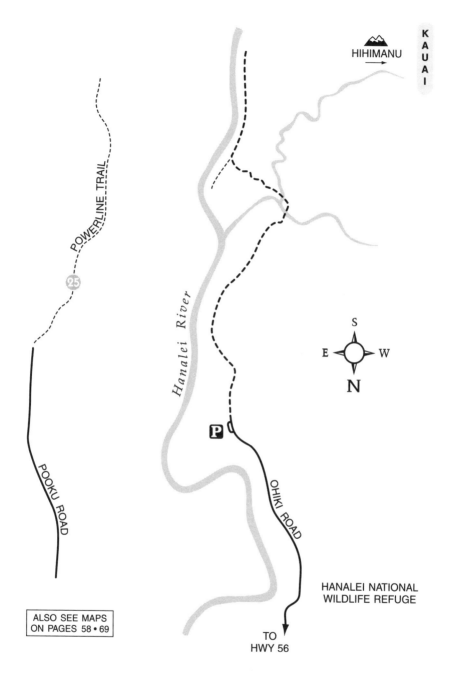

HIHIMANU

K A U A I

POWERLINE TRAIL

25

Hanalei River

POOKU ROAD

P

OHIKI ROAD

S

E ⊕ W

N

HANALEI NATIONAL
WILDLIFE REFUGE

TO
HWY 56

ALSO SEE MAPS
ON PAGES 58 • 69

# HANALEI RIVER TRAIL

# Hike 29
# Kee Beach to Hanakapiai Beach
## KALALAU TRAIL ON NA PALI COAST

**Hiking distance:** 4 miles round trip
**Hiking time:** 2 hours
**Elevation gain:** 1,000 feet
**Maps:** U.S.G.S. Haena

**Summary of hike:** The Kalalau Trail along the Na Pali Coast is an undeveloped, ancient Hawaiian route accessible only by foot. The 11-mile trail follows the Na Pali Coast along the edge of massive, windswept cliffs to Kalalau Beach. The rugged coastline hike overlooks a series of primeval, emerald green valleys and steep towering cliffs that drop more than 3,000 feet to the turbulent sea. This unforgettable hike covers the first two miles of the trail to Hanakapiai Beach at the mouth of Hanakapiai Valley, the first valley leading to the island's interior. To head up the valley, continue on Hike 30.

**Driving directions:** Follow driving directions for Hike 30 to Kee Beach.

**Hiking directions:** The signed trail begins on the inland side of the road by a large map and history exhibit. The uneven lava rock path, which is usually wet and sometimes slippery, immediately climbs through the lush tropical vegetation. In the first half mile, numerous vista points overlook Kee Beach, the scalloped Na Pali coastline, and the precipitous cliffs dropping off into the fierce, pounding surf. Continue steadily uphill, traversing the cliffs for one mile. The trail levels out, and at 1.5 miles, begins to descend towards Hanakapiai Beach. Short, steep switchbacks lead down to the stream past tsunami warning signs. Cross Hanakapiai Stream at the white sand beach to a signed junction. This is our turnaround spot.

To hike further, the right fork climbs out of the valley and continues on the Kalalau Trail (permit required). Hike 30 follows the Hanakapiai Falls Trail to the left to a beautiful waterfall.

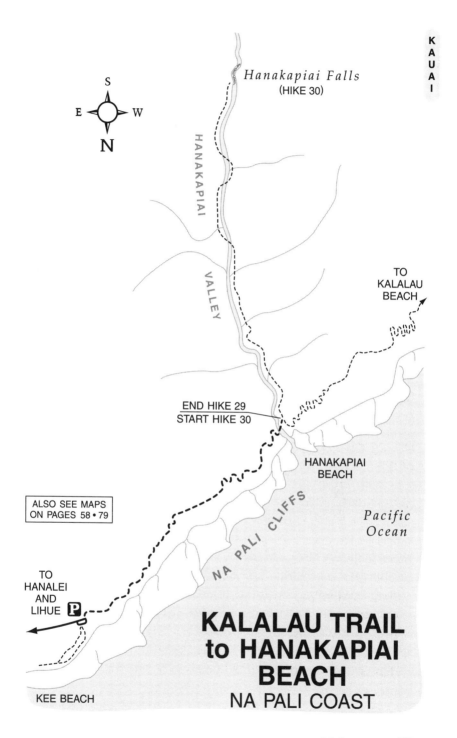

S
E · W
N

K A U A I

*Hanakapiai Falls*
(HIKE 30)

HANAKAPIAI

VALLEY

TO
KALALAU
BEACH

END HIKE 29
START HIKE 30

HANAKAPIAI
BEACH

ALSO SEE MAPS
ON PAGES 58 • 79

NA PALI CLIFFS

*Pacific
Ocean*

TO
HANALEI
AND
LIHUE  P

KALALAU TRAIL
to HANAKAPIAI
BEACH
NA PALI COAST

KEE BEACH

# Hike 30
# Hanakapiai Beach to Hanakapiai Falls
## KALALAU TRAIL ON NA PALI COAST

**Hiking distance:** 8 miles round trip (from Kee Beach)
**Hiking time:** 5 hours
**Elevation gain:** 1,750 feet
**Maps:** U.S.G.S. Haena
       Northwestern Kauai Recreation Map

**Summary of hike:** The Hanakapiai Falls Trail begins two miles up the Kalalau Trail on the Na Pali Coast at Hanakapiai Beach—the turnaround spot for Hike 29. This side trail leads up Hanakapiai Valley, a steep-walled, stream-fed valley, to a 300-foot cataract and pool in a natural amphitheater. Along the way there are stream crossings and additional swimming pools.

**Driving directions:** From Lihue, drive 37 miles north and west on Highway 56 past Hanalei to the end of the road. At Princeville the mile markers begin again at 1. Park on the right side of the road at mile marker 10 in the Kee Beach parking area. Along the way, the road hugs the coast past ocean bays, caves, streams, waterfalls, and crosses numerous one-lane bridges.

**Hiking directions:** Follow the hiking directions for Hike 29 to Hanakapiai Beach (2 miles). Take the left fork, heading inland into the sheltered Hanakapiai Valley. The first mile follows the west bank of the Hanakapiai Stream to a sheltered picnic table, passing huge mango trees. Soon the trail crosses the stream and becomes more difficult to hike due to mud, erosion, and stream crossings. At 1.7 miles is a large pool and two consecutive stream crossings. Continue up the narrow valley along the east bank of the stream past several small waterfalls and pools. The trail ends at the base of Hanakapiai Falls and a pool surrounded by large boulders. Mist from the falls sprays onto the thick vegetation and moss-covered rocks. Return along the same trail.

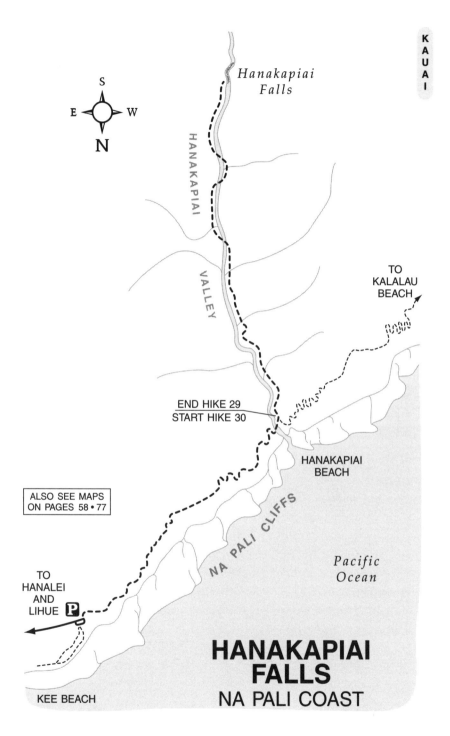

S
E ✦ W
N

KAUAI

*Hanakapiai
Falls*

HANAKAPIAI

VALLEY

TO
KALALAU
BEACH

END HIKE 29
START HIKE 30

HANAKAPIAI
BEACH

ALSO SEE MAPS
ON PAGES 58 • 77

NA PALI CLIFFS

*Pacific
Ocean*

TO
HANALEI
AND
LIHUE  P

# HANAKAPIAI
# FALLS
## NA PALI COAST

KEE BEACH

# Maui

# Island of Maui

Many of Maui's most beautiful and unique attractions are easily accessible by foot. These 30 hikes on Maui take you to the island's best hikes, including the entire coastline and the upcountry regions of West Maui and Haleakala National Park. An overall map of Maui and the locations of the hikes is found on the next page. The hikes are roughly divided into coastal hikes, the upcountry, and the Hana Highway.

Geographically, Maui is surprisingly diverse. Within an hour you may go from verdant, humid rain forests to the stark, cold, and fascinating lunar landscape of the Haleakala crater. Hikes range from gentle beach strolls along the undulating coastline to steep mountain trails with sweeping views of the entire island. A quick glance at the hikes' summaries will allow you to choose a hike that is appropriate to your ability and desire. These areas may be enjoyed for a short time or the whole day.

Visions of Hawaii often include temperate sandy beaches, crystal-clear tidepools, secluded coves, and the surf crashing into a jagged lava coastline. You will find just such a landscape along the coastal hikes in West Maui and the island's southwest perimeter (Hikes 1—14). Explore world-class beaches, sea caves, turquoise ocean bays, lava flows, dormant cones, ancient Hawaiian sites, and steep canyons with waterfalls. Traveling just a few miles inland leads to West Maui's emerald green interior, including the mossy mantle of the Iao Needle.

On the island's east lobe, the upcountry region includes Polipoli State Park in a quiet, meditative forest with an understory of ferns and mosses. Extensive trails cross through this forest reserve on the west slopes of Haleakala and connect with the volcano's summit (Hikes 15—18).

To the west of this state park is Haleakala National Park, extending from the 10,023-foot summit of Maui to the coastline. The unique park is embraces the world's largest dormant volcano—Haleakala. Several trails lead into this magnificent area, from the crater rim to the barren landscape of the crater floor (Hikes 19—22).

One of the most scenic drives in all Hawaii is along the Hana Highway. This gorgeous, winding 55-mile road traverses the northeast slopes of Haleakala along the edge of the windward coastal cliffs. Hikes 24—30 are found along this road. Highlights include waterfalls, freshwater swimming pools, deep canyons, seascape vistas, over 600 curves, and more than fifty one-lane bridges. After visiting the charming town of Hana, the road continues to Oheo Gulch, where the flows of Haleakala once spilled into the ocean. A series of descending pools cascade into each other through this gulch before emerging with the Pacific out of a rock grotto (Hikes 29 and 30).

The thought of exploring Maui may cause you to don tank tops and sandals. Winds, high elevations, wet rain forests, and dry deserts will make it necessary to have a variety of clothing when exploring Maui. Bring hats (for both hot and cool weather), jackets, and gloves. Sunscreen, insect repellent, sunglasses, drinking water, and snacks are a must. Elevations are as high as 10,000 feet and surprisingly chilly. Warm clothing will be required when exploring the peaks and valleys of Haleakala. Also bring swimwear and outdoor gear to enjoy the coastal areas for the day.

Your time on Maui will be enhanced by exploring Maui's unique geography. Enjoy the trails!

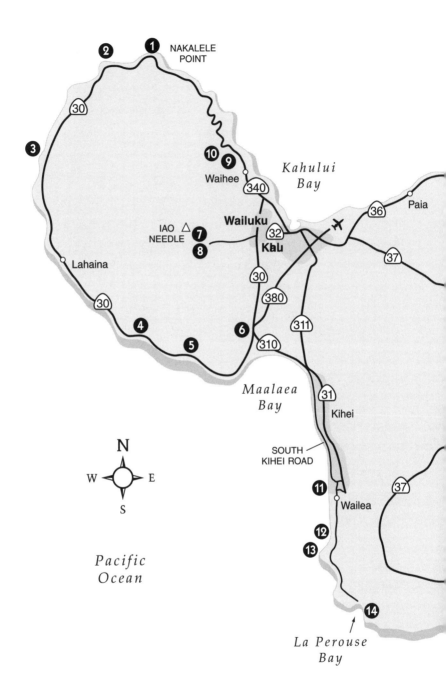

NAKALELE
POINT

30

Kahului
Bay

Waihee

340

Paia

36

IAO △
NEEDLE

Wailuku

32

Kahu

Lahaina

30

30

380

311

37

310

Maalaea
Bay

31

Kihei

SOUTH
KIHEI ROAD

N
W ◇ E
S

Wailea

37

Pacific
Ocean

La Perouse
Bay

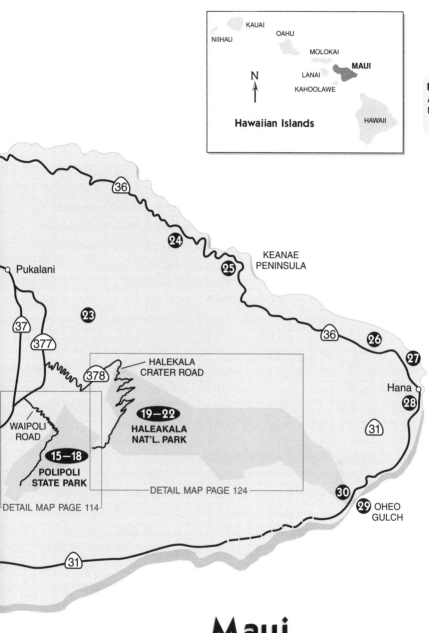

KAUAI
NIIHAU
OAHU
MOLOKAI
**MAUI**
N
LANAI
KAHOOLAWE
HAWAII

**Hawaiian Islands**

M
A
U
I

36

24

KEANAE
PENINSULA

Pukalani

25

23

37

377

36

26

378

27

HALEKALA
CRATER ROAD

Hana

28

**19—22**
**HALEAKALA**
**NAT'L. PARK**

WAIPOLI
ROAD

31

**15—18**
**POLIPOLI**
**STATE PARK**

DETAIL MAP PAGE 124

30

DETAIL MAP PAGE 114

29 OHEO
GULCH

31

# Maui
# MAP OF THE HIKES

# Hike 1
## Nakalele Blowhole

**Hiking distance:** 1 mile round trip
**Hiking time:** 1 hour
**Elevation gain:** 200 feet
**Maps:** U.S.G.S. Napili
       Maui Recreation Map

**Summary of hike:** This place is pure magic. The Nakalele Blowhole is at the desolate north tip of Maui by a lighthouse beacon on the east edge of Nakalele Point. The blowhole is in a small cove with rough, turbulent surf. The cove is surrounded by layered, wind-sculpted lava formations and tidepools. At the trailhead is a surrealistic open field covered with hundreds of cairns. The trail passes the light beacon before crossing the beautifully carved lava rock shelf, passing tidepools en route to the blowhole. The blowhole erupts as incoming waves blast air and water through a hole from an underwater sea cave. The water will spurt more vigorously during high tide.

**Driving directions:** From Lahaina, drive 16 miles north on Highway 30 to the north tip of the island. Park on the left (ocean side) of the road at a large open area marked by a sign.

**Hiking directions:** Follow the old jeep road/trail as it winds into the ironwood tree grove. Continue the gradual descent east past the Coast Guard beacon and down to the ocean. The path ends beyond the beacon. Walk out over the lava shelf past tidepools towards the farthest point. The blowhole is in a cove east of Nakalele Point. If you have any difficulty locating the blowhole, listen for the frequent eruptions. Explore the amazing jagged landscape along your own route.

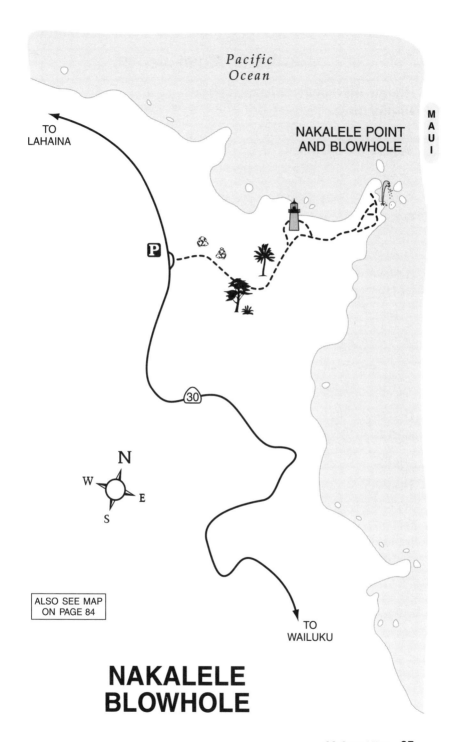

Pacific
Ocean

TO
LAHAINA

NAKALELE POINT
AND BLOWHOLE

M
A
U
I

P

30

N
W    E
S

ALSO SEE MAP
ON PAGE 84

TO
WAILUKU

# NAKALELE BLOWHOLE

# Hike 2
# Lipoa Point

**Hiking distance:** 1 mile round trip
**Hiking time:** 30 minutes
**Elevation gain:** 100 feet
**Maps:** U.S.G.S. Napili

**Summary of hike:** At Lipoa Point are tidepools, hollowed out caves, arches, and clear snorkeling and soaking pools. The point is at the northwest tip of Kulaokaea, a large plateau used for cultivating pineapples. The broad, flat plateau, known locally as Golf Links, was the site of a golf course in the 1940s. A few eroded trails also lead down the steep cliffs into small pocket beaches in Honolua Bay, a designated marine sanctuary.

**Driving directions:** From Lahaina, drive 11.8 miles north on Highway 30 to a wide red dirt road on the left, between mile markers 33 and 34. The highway curves to the right at the turnoff. Turn left and follow the road along the west side of Lipoa Point through pineapple fields. The end of the road is at 0.3 miles. Along the way are several pullouts on the left that lead to steep trails descending the cliffs into Honolua Bay.

**Hiking directions:** From the pullouts before the end of the road, the path zigzags down the steep cliffs to a knoll and trail junction. The left fork leads down to the north end of Honolua Bay. To the right, an equally steep trail descends into a small pocket cove. Use caution and good judgement to descend.

From the main trail at the end of the road, follow the red dirt path along the perimeter of the plateau towards Lipoa Point. Several side paths descend to the left. At 0.3 miles are the remains of an old rock wall, the site of the golf course clubhouse. Near the wall is a Norfolk pine grove and a trail junction. Bear left and descend the hill towards Lipoa Point. Various paths crisscross the lava rock point that overlooks the jagged coastline and interesting rock formations. Explore along your own route.

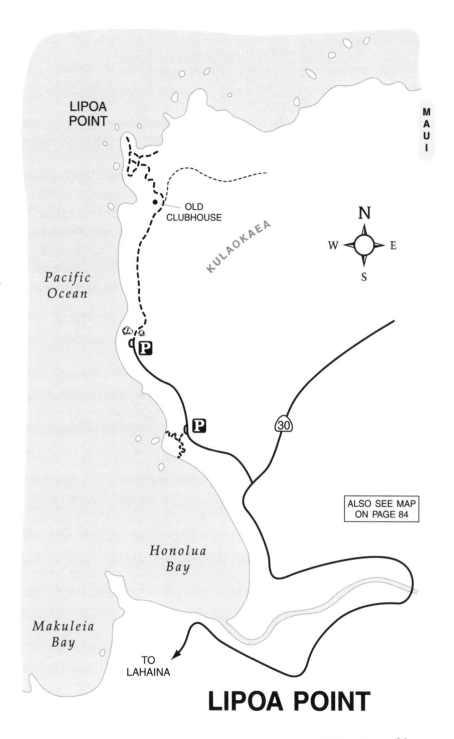

LIPOA
POINT

MAUI

OLD
CLUBHOUSE

KULAOKAEA

N
W E
S

Pacific
Ocean

P

P

30

ALSO SEE MAP
ON PAGE 84

Honolua
Bay

Makuleia
Bay

TO
LAHAINA

# LIPOA POINT

# Hike 3
## D.T. Fleming Beach Park
## to Makaluapuna Point

**Hiking distance:** 1.5 miles round trip
**Hiking time:** 1 hour
**Elevation gain:** Level
**Maps:** U.S.G.S. Napili
Maui Recreation Map

**Summary of hike:** Fleming Beach Park is a crescent-shaped beach protected by two rocky headlands at Honokahua Bay. Honokahua Stream empties into the bay in a grove of ironwood and kiawe trees. Makaluapuna Point is the lava rock peninsula jutting a quarter mile into the ocean, separating Honokahua Bay from Oneloa Bay. A ridge of jagged trachyte formations known as "Dragon's Teeth" extend to the point. The hike begins at the beach and leads across the lava formations to the point, exploring tidepools and overlooking the crashing surf. East Molokai is visible across the Pailolo Channel.

**Driving directions:** From Lahaina, drive about 10 miles north on Highway 30 to the north end of Kapalua. Turn left to the D.T. Fleming Beach Park parking lot.

**Hiking directions:** From the sandy beach, walk to the left (west) along the crescent of sand. The sand ends at the foot of Makaluapuna Point. Begin climbing the field of lava rocks towards the distinct trachyte formations. Continue along the side of the jagged ridge, working your way to Makaluapuna Point. (The Kapalua Golf Course boundary eliminates direct access into Oneloa Bay.) After exploring this magnificent area, return the way you came.

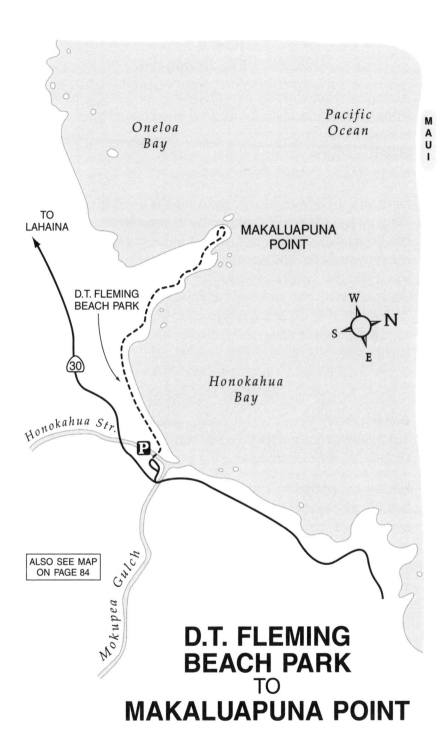

Oneloa Bay

Pacific Ocean

MAUI

TO LAHAINA

MAKALUAPUNA POINT

D.T. FLEMING BEACH PARK

30

Honokahua Str.

P

Honokahua Bay

W N S E

ALSO SEE MAP ON PAGE 84

Mokupea Gulch

# D.T. FLEMING BEACH PARK TO MAKALUAPUNA POINT

# Hike 4
# Olowalu Petroglyphs

**Hiking distance:** 1 mile round trip
**Hiking time:** 1 hour
**Elevation gain:** 100 feet
**Maps:** U.S.G.S. Olowalu
       Map of Maui—The Valley Isle

**Summary of hike:** The Olowalu Petroglyphs are ancient Hawaiian petroglyphs (images chiseled into the rock surface) depicting humans and animals. The 300-year-old stone carvings are engraved into the face of Kilea, a volcanic cinder cone in the V-shaped Olowalu Valley. The trail follows an ancient Hawaiian route that crossed the Olowalu Valley into the Iao Valley. This area is now privately owned, and public access ends at the petroglyphs.

**Driving directions:** From Lahaina, drive 6 miles south on Highway 30 to the Olowalu Store on the inland (left) side of the highway, near mile marker 15. Turn left and park near but not in front of the store.

From Wailuku, drive south on Highway 30. Curve west around McGregor Point towards Lahaina, reaching the Olowalu Store on the right at about 15 miles.

**Hiking directions:** Walk behind the Olowalu Store and down the cane road to the water tank. Follow the dirt road for a half mile through the sugar cane field into the Olowalu Valley towards Kilea, the volcanic hill. As the road approaches the distinct cinder cone, human figures carved into the face of the west hillside will be visible. Unstable remnants of walkways, railings, and an observation platform remain. After viewing the petroglyphs, you must return along the same route. Further access on the privately owned road is prohibited.

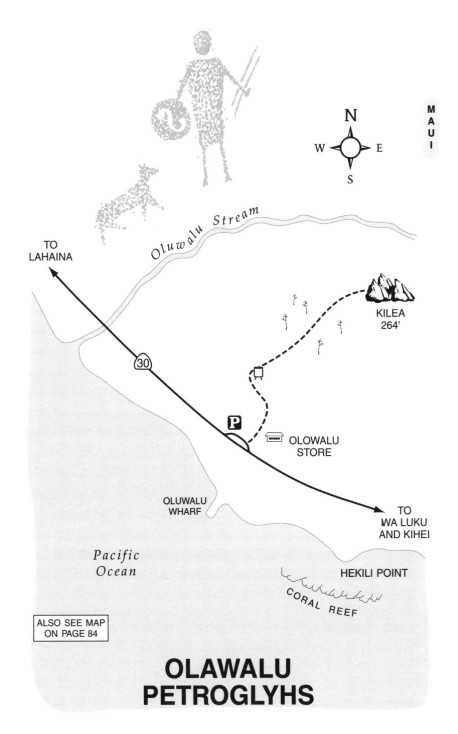

N
W E
S

MAUI

Oluwalu Stream

TO
LAHAINA

30

KILEA
264'

P

OLOWALU
STORE

OLUWALU
WHARF

TO
WA LUKU
AND KIHEI

Pacific
Ocean

HEKILI POINT

CORAL REEF

ALSO SEE MAP
ON PAGE 84

# OLAWALU
# PETROGLYHS

# Hike 5
## Lahaina Pali Trail
### FROM THE UKUMEHAME (WEST) TRAILHEAD

**Hiking distance:** 5 miles round trip
**Hiking time:** 3 hours
**Elevation gain:** 1,600 feet
**Maps:** U.S.G.S. Maalaea
The Lahaina Pali Trail Guide

map
next page

**Summary of hike:** The Lahaina Pali Trail is an old Hawaiian horse and foot trail built in the early 1800s. The trail was used as a more direct route across the arid southern slopes of the West Maui Mountains, connecting Lahaina and Olowalu with Maalaea and Wailuku. There are two trailheads that zigzag up the mountain, crossing ridges and gullies to the 1,600-foot ridge. The interpretive trail passes rock outcroppings, ancient stone walls, and offers panoramic coastal vistas of Lanai, Kahoolawe, Haleakala, and the Molokini Islands. This hike begins from the Ukumehame (West) Trailhead and can be combined with Hike 6 for a one-way, 5-mile shuttle hike.

**Driving directions:** The signed trailhead is on the inland side of the Kahekili Highway (30) between the 10 and 11 mile marker. It is 4 miles west of the Maalaea Harbor and a half mile past the Lahaina Tunnel. It is 10 miles southeast of downtown Lahaina. Turn inland and park in the trailhead parking area under the shade of the kiawe trees.

**Hiking directions:** Walk through the grove and up the steps to the mouth of Manawaipueo Gulch. Bear right on the asphalt road, the old, winding carriage route used before the Highway 30 tunnel was built. Head to the signed footpath 60 yards ahead. Bear left on the Lahaina Pali Trail, ascending the mountain to the west edge of Kamaohi Gulch. The highway tunnel can be seen at the mouth of the gulch. Follow the cliff's edge to the head of the gulch and cross. Watch for a cave on the left. The trail heads up and crosses Mokumana Gulch at one mile and

Opunaha Gulch at 1.4 miles. A water trough for cattle is on the right. The path levels out after crossing Makahuna Gulch. Views extend down the Kihei coastline to the offshore islands and the towering Haleakala. Cross Kaalaina Gulch to the open expanse of Pohakuloa. Descend to the base of Manawainui Gulch to the shade of a wiliwili tree at 1.9 miles. Climb back out on the switchbacks to the high point of the trail on the windswept ridge by signpost 10. This is our turnaround spot. To hike further, the trail descends to the Maalaea Trailhead (Hike 6).

# Hike 6
# Lahaina Pali Trail
## FROM THE MAALAEA (EAST) TRAILHEAD

**Hiking distance:** 5 miles round trip
**Hiking time:** 3 hours
**Elevation gain:** 1,600 feet
**Maps:** U.S.G.S. Maalaea
The Lahaina Pali Trail Guide

map
next page

**Summary of hike:** The Lahaina Pali Trail is an old route across the southern end of the West Maui Mountains, connecting Lahaina with Maalaea and Wailuku. The serpentine horse and foot trail was hand built in the early 1800s. The path crosses numerous ridges and gullies, reaching the 1,600 foot summit on a windswept ridge. This hike begins from the Maalaea (East) Trailhead and can be combined with Hike 5 for a one-way, 5-mile shuttle hike. The interpretive trail passes rock outcroppings, ancient stone walls, and trail paving stones while offering access to sweeping coastal and island views.

**Driving directions:** The signed trailhead is on the Kahekili Highway (30) at the north end of Kihei by Maalaea. The trailhead is 0.1 mile south of the Kuihelani Highway (380) and 0.2 miles north of the North Kihei Road (310) on the west side of the road. Turn west off Highway 30 to the signed trailhead gate. Drive through the gate, closing the gate, and continue 0.2 miles to a junction. Bear left and follow the trail signs. Cross through another gate, driving 0.6 miles to the parking area on the right.

**Hiking directions:** Walk through the entrance gate, and follow the rock-lined path through groves of kiawe trees. Begin climbing up the steep path, zigzagging up the ridge of the mountain while leaving the shade behind. Views unfold of Maui and the surrounding islands. Traverse the mountainside, crossing numerous dry gullies. Continue steadily uphill. The trail levels out on Kealaloloa Ridge. Curve around the ridge to the McGregor Point Jeep Trail, an unpaved road at the edge of Malalowaiaole Gulch. Take the road to the left, crossing the gulch to a signed junction. Leave the road and take the footpath to the right. Climb up the rock steps to the high point of the trail on a ridge by signpost 10. This is our turnaround spot. To hike further, the trail descends to the Ukumehame Trailhead (Hike 5).

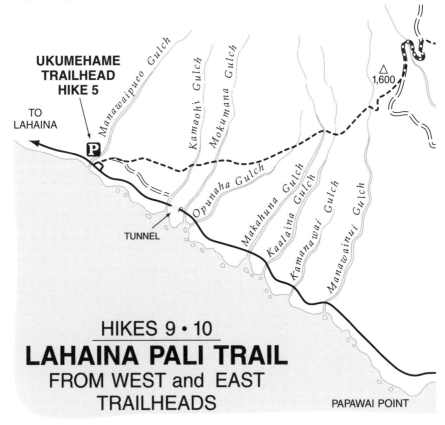

HIKES 9 • 10
# LAHAINA PALI TRAIL
## FROM WEST and EAST
## TRAILHEADS

PAPAWAI POINT

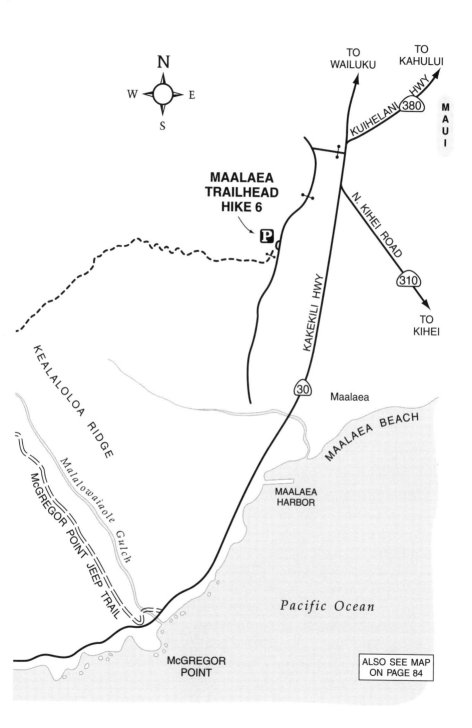

# Hike 7
# Iao Needle Overlook and Botanical Garden
## IAO VALLEY STATE PARK

**Hiking distance:** 0.6 miles round trip
**Hiking time:** 30 minutes
**Elevation gain:** 150 feet
**Maps:** U.S.G.S. Wailuku

**Summary of hike:** Iao Valley, an ancient sacred site and spiritual center, sits in a rich green chasm in the West Maui Mountains above the town of Wailuku. The six-acre state park is home of Kukaemoku, commonly referred to as the Iao Needle, a moss-covered 2,250-foot basalt mantle that sharply rises 1,200 feet from the valley floor. The Iao Needle Overlook is a roofed pavilion with benches overlooking Wailuku, the Iao Valley, Iao Needle, and the precipitous steep valley walls. A paved nature trail curves through a tropical botanic garden that borders the banks of the Iao Stream. The gardens are landscaped with native and introduced plants.

**Driving directions:** Iao Valley State Park is at the west end of Wailuku. From downtown, turn west (towards the mountains) on Main Street/Highway 32. Drive 2.8 miles to the end of the road and park in the lot.

**Hiking directions:** Hike up the paved path past the restrooms towards the bridge crossing over a tributary of Iao Stream. Before crossing, take the interpretive nature trail to the left, descending into the botanical garden. Follow the paved path, exploring the gardens and ponds. The trail loops at the southern end along Iao Stream. After strolling through the gardens, return to the main trail by the bridge. Cross the bridge over the stream and curve left on the paved path to a trail split. The left fork leads to the Streamside Trail (Hike 8). Take the right fork and ascend over a hundred steps to the Iao Needle Overlook shelter at the end of the trail.

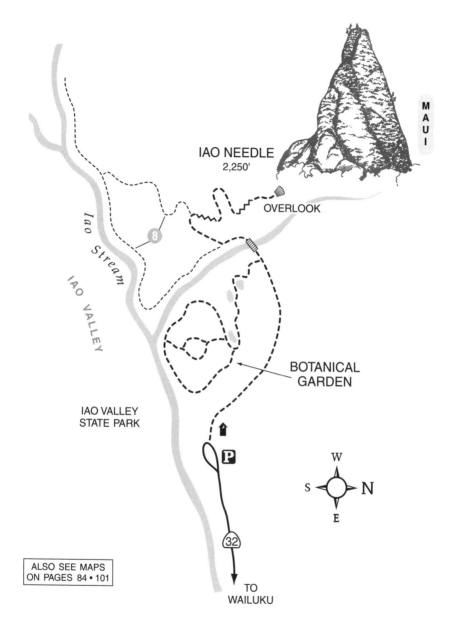

IAO NEEDLE
2,250'

MAUI

OVERLOOK

Iao Stream

IAO VALLEY

8

BOTANICAL
GARDEN

IAO VALLEY
STATE PARK

P

W
S N
E

32

ALSO SEE MAPS
ON PAGES 84 • 101

TO
WAILUKU

# IAO NEEDLE OVERLOOK
## BOTANICAL GARDEN
### IAO VALLEY STATE PARK

# Hike 8
# Streamside Trail
## IAO VALLEY STATE PARK

**Hiking distance:** 1 mile round trip
**Hiking time:** 30 minutes
**Elevation gain:** 200 feet
**Maps:** U.S.G.S. Wailuku

**Summary of hike:** The Streamside Trail meanders through the lush stream-fed chasm and dramatic landscape of Iao Valley State Park, an ancient spiritual center in the West Maui Mountains. Waters from a network of tributary streams emerge from the folds of Iao Valley, converging inside the park to form Iao Stream. The trail crosses a footbridge over a stream and winds through a shady tropical forest to tumbling cascades, small waterfalls, and natural pools.

**Driving directions:** Iao Valley State Park is at the west end of Wailuku. From downtown, turn west (towards the mountains) on Main Street/Highway 32. Drive 2.8 miles to the end of the road and park in the lot.

**Hiking directions:** Walk up the paved path past the restrooms to a bridge crossing a tributary of Iao Stream. From the bridge is an excellent view of the 2,250-foot Iao Needle. After crossing, curve left to a trail split. The right fork leads up to the Iao Needle Overlook (Hike 7). Bear left and descend to the Iao Stream. Follow the paved path along the stream as the cascading whitewater tumbles over rocks. When the paved path loops to the right, away from the stream, watch for a streamside footpath heading west. Follow the footpath upstream into the damp forest, passing cascades to several pools. Use caution as the mossy rocks are slippery. Return to the paved path. Take the left fork and ascend the hill through guava and yellow ginger trees to a junction. The left fork climbs steps to the Iao Needle Overlook (Hike 7). Stay to the right and complete the loop. Return to the left.

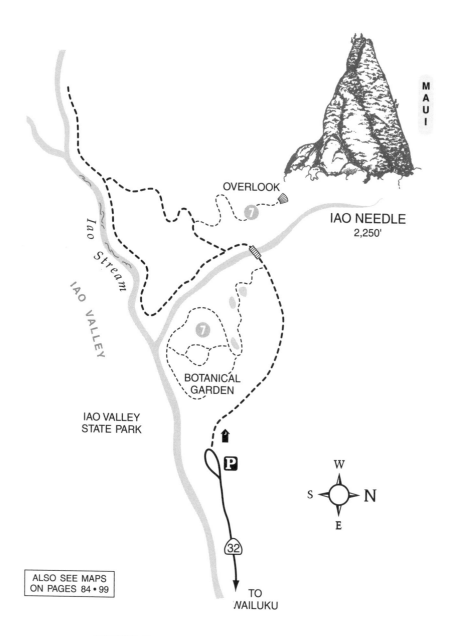

MAUI

OVERLOOK

IAO NEEDLE
2,250'

Iao Stream

IAO VALLEY

BOTANICAL
GARDEN

IAO VALLEY
STATE PARK

P

W
S + N
E

ALSO SEE MAPS
ON PAGES 84 • 99

32

TO
WAILUKU

# STREAMSIDE TRAIL
## IAO VALLEY STATE PARK

# Hike 9
# Waihee Valley

Hiking permit needed from Wailuku Agribusiness
Call (808) 244-9570

**Hiking distance:** 4 miles round trip
**Hiking time:** 2 hours
**Elevation gain:** 300 feet
**Maps:** U.S.G.S. Wailuku

**Summary of hike:** Waihee Valley is a narrow, stream-fed canyon with steep vertical walls. The trail winds gently through the lush, tropical rain forest and crosses two long swinging bridges over the Waihee River. The hike winds up the canyon past bamboo forests, huge banyan trees, and views of narrow waterfalls cascading over the steep canyon walls. Be aware that flash flooding is possible. If it is raining, do not hike in this area.

**Driving directions:** From the intersection of Main Street and Market Street in downtown Wailuku, head north on Market Street. Veer to the left onto Highway 340 and drive through the town of Waihee. From the Waihee School on the left, continue 0.5 miles to the signed Waihee Valley Road and turn left. Drive 0.5 miles to the end of the road and park.

**Hiking directions:** At the end of Waihee Valley Road, walk on the service road to the right (west). As you pass some abandoned cars, water can be heard flowing through an irrigation ditch. Follow the irrigation stream through the lush forest as it flows in and out of tunnels dug into the cliffs. At one mile, cross the first swinging bridge. The riverbed may be dry depending on where the water is being diverted from the irrigation system. Crossing the bridges is great fun regardless of the water level. After crossing, bear left to a second bridge. Continue up the canyon to where the trail fords the river. This is a good turnaround spot if you do not wish to wade through the water. To hike further, the trail fords the river a second time, reaching the dam and swimming holes in less than a half mile.

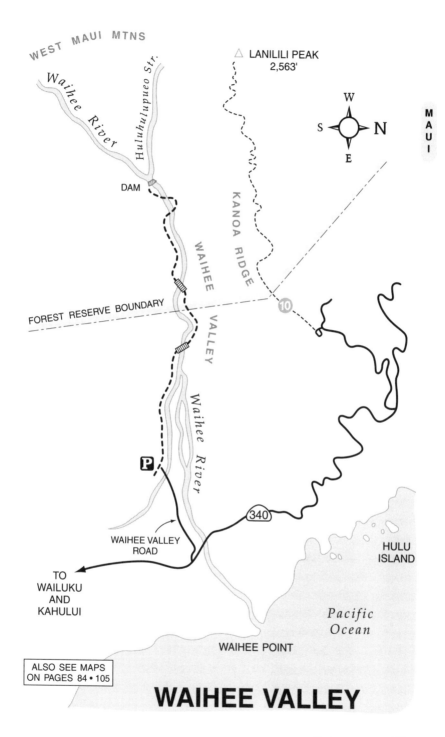

WEST MAUI MTNS

Waihee River

Huluhulupueo Str.

△ LANILILI PEAK
2,563'

W
S ✦ N
E

M
A
U
I

DAM

KANOA RIDGE

WAIHEE VALLEY

FOREST RESERVE BOUNDARY

10

Waihee River

P

Waihee River

340

HULU
ISLAND

WAIHEE VALLEY
ROAD

TO
WAILUKU
AND
KAHULUI

Pacific
Ocean

WAIHEE POINT

ALSO SEE MAPS
ON PAGES 84 • 105

# WAIHEE VALLEY

# Hike 10
# Waihee Ridge

**Hiking distance:** 4.5 miles round trip
**Hiking time:** 2.5 hours
**Elevation gain:** 1,500 feet
**Maps:** U.S.G.S. Wailuku
   Island of Maui Recreation Map

**Summary of hike:** The Waihee Ridge Trail begins in the rolling pasturelands of the West Maui Mountains. The trail climbs the windward slopes along the crest of Kanoa Ridge overlooking the Waihee Canyon (Hike 9). The path leads through the heavily foliated rainforest to Lanilili Peak. There are incredible views along the way of the canyons, mountain ridges, and coastline. The trail is well maintained but portions are wet and muddy.

**Driving directions:** From the intersection of Main Street and Market Street in downtown Wailuku, head north on Market Street. Veer to the left onto Highway 340 and drive through the town of Waihee. From the Waihee School on the left, continue 2.7 miles to the signed Camp Maluhia turnoff and turn left. Drive 0.8 miles to the grassy parking area on the left by the vehicle gate.

**Hiking directions:** Hike west past the trailhead gate, and proceed 0.2 miles through the pastureland. Walk up the steep concrete right-of-way road towards a water tower on the right. Take the signed grassy footpath uphill to the left. At a quarter mile, cross through the forest reserve gate. Continue uphill through the rainforest to an overlook on a saddle at 0.5 miles. Long switchbacks lead up the mountain to a second saddle with great views into Waihee Valley and the Maui isthmus. More switchbacks ascend the mountain to a narrow ridge. At 1.5 miles, the trail levels and crosses a meadow towards Lanilili Peak. Switchbacks lead up to the 2,563-foot summit, a grassy hilltop with a picnic table at trail's end. After viewing the massive ridges and deep valleys, return by retracing your steps.

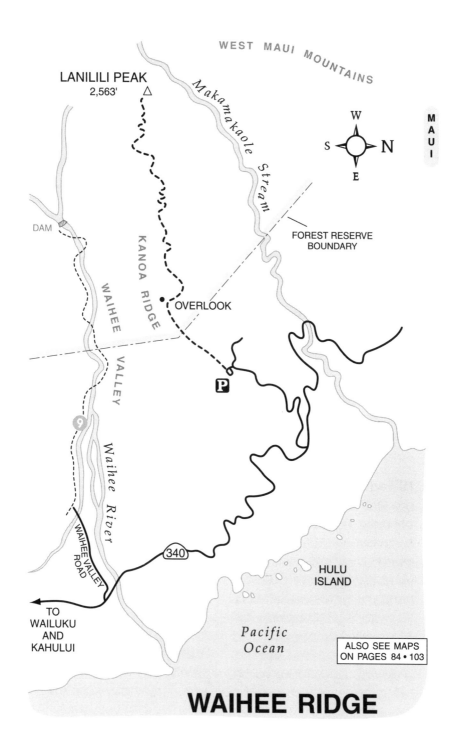

LANILILI PEAK
2,563'

WEST MAUI MOUNTAINS

Makamakaole Stream

MAUI

W
S · N
E

FOREST RESERVE
BOUNDARY

KANOA RIDGE

DAM

WAIHEE VALLEY

OVERLOOK

P

9

Waihee River

WAIHEE VALLEY ROAD

340

HULU
ISLAND

TO
WAILUKU
AND
KAHULUI

Pacific
Ocean

ALSO SEE MAPS
ON PAGES 84 • 103

# WAIHEE RIDGE

# Hike 11
## Wailea Oceanfront Boardwalk
### Keawakapu, Mokapu, Ulua, Wailea, and Polo Beaches

**Hiking distance:** 4 miles round trip
**Hiking time:** 2 hours
**Elevation gain:** Level
**Maps:** U.S.G.S. Makena

**Summary of hike:** The Wailea Boardwalk follows two miles of coastline fronting a string of world class resorts. Each of the five public beaches have differing characteristics; all are great swimming and snorkeling sites. The lush, landscaped grounds of the resorts behind the beaches are also a treasure to explore. The boardwalk connects the five beach coves, which are separated by wide stretches of lava rock promontories with tide-pools. The Hawaiian Coastal Gardens on Wailea Point are a half-mile long with over 60 native plants. Throughout the hike are great views of Molokini Island, Kahoolawe, and Lanai.

**Driving directions:** At the south end of Kihei, the South Kihei Road ends. Where the main road curves left at the signed entrance to Wailea on Okolani Drive, take the right fork 0.2 miles to the Keawakapu Beach parking lot at the road's end.

**Hiking directions:** Walk down the steps to Keawakapu Beach. Bear left between the kiawe trees on the sand dunes and the oceanfront lava rocks. Follow the sandy strand 0.2 miles to the paved walking path in front of the Wailea Beach Resort at Mokapu Beach. Wind through the landscaped gardens with spur paths leading to the oceanfront and tidepools. The boardwalk continues to Wailea Elua Village and Ulua Beach along the weaving contours of the landscaped grounds. Cross the lava formations and tidepools to the Outrigger Wailea Resort, then the Grand Wailea Resort fronted by Wailea Beach. Head up the grassy bluffs to the Hawaiian Coastal Gardens. Cross the footbridge over the lush gully to the rocky cliffs of Wailea Point. Around the point, pass the remains of an ancient Hawaiian home

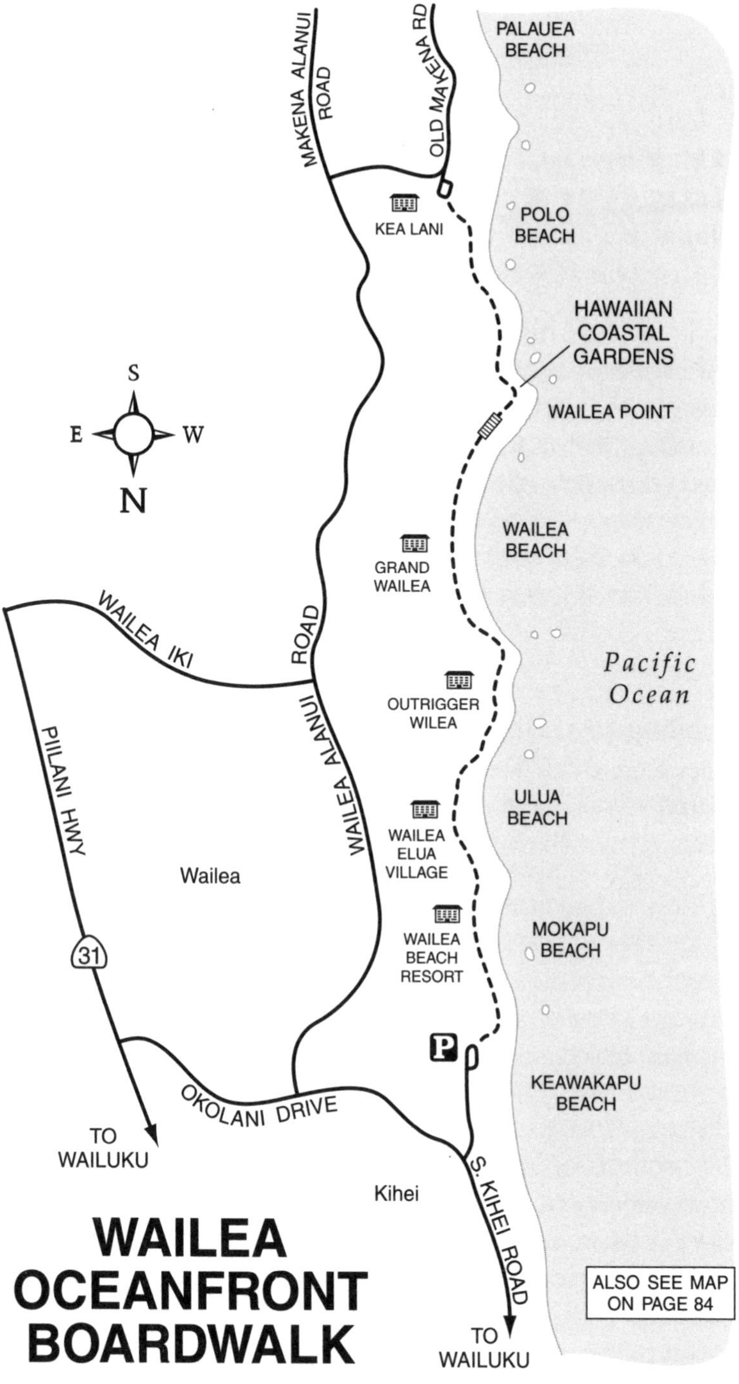

MAKENA ALANUI ROAD

OLD MAKENA RD

PALAUEA BEACH

M A U I

KEA LANI

POLO BEACH

HAWAIIAN COASTAL GARDENS

WAILEA POINT

S

E ✦ W

N

GRAND WAILEA

WAILEA BEACH

WAILEA IKI

*Pacific Ocean*

WAILEA ALANUI ROAD

OUTRIGGER WILEA

PIILANI HWY

ULUA BEACH

Wailea

WAILEA ELUA VILLAGE

31

WAILEA BEACH RESORT

MOKAPU BEACH

P

KEAWAKAPU BEACH

OKOLANI DRIVE

TO WAILUKU

Kihei

S. KIHEI ROAD

# WAILEA
# OCEANFRONT
# BOARDWALK

TO WAILUKU

ALSO SEE MAP ON PAGE 84

# Hike 12
# Maluaka Beach

**Hiking distance:** 1.2 miles round trip
**Hiking time:** 40 minutes
**Elevation gain:** Level
**Maps:** U.S.G.S. Makena
        Island Of Maui Recreation Map

**Summary of hike:** Maluaka Beach is a small sandy beach in Makena Bay bordered to the north by Keawalai Point. The beach is adjacent to Keawalai Church, founded in 1832, and the historic graveyard. The protected beach cove is backed by sand dunes and kiawe trees. On the grassy bluffs to the south is a landscaped park, picnic area, and the Maui Prince Hotel. The low rocky bluffs of Maluaka Point separate the beach from the black sand of Oneuli Beach. From the bluffs are gorgeous views of the coastline.

**Driving directions:** At the south end of Kihei, the South Kihei Road ends. The road curves left at the signed entrance to Wailea on Okolani Drive. Go one block to the junction with Wailea Alanui Road on the right. Turn right and drive 3 miles south to Makena Road. (Wailea Alanui Road becomes Makena Alanui Road along the way.) Turn right and continue 0.8 miles to the parking lot on the left, across the road from the historic Keawalai Church.

A second parking lot is is at the south end of the beach near Maluaka Point. Access is on an unmarked turnoff from Makena Alanui Road, shortly after passing the Maui Prince Hotel.

**Hiking directions:** From the Makena Road parking lot, walk a short distance south on the road to the Maluaka Beach access near the end of the road. Follow the tree-lined crescent of sand to the south end of the bay. Climb up the grassy bluffs by the Maui Prince Hotel. Steps lead up to the grassy knoll and picnic area landscaped with trees. Cross the knoll southwest towards Maluaka Point. Hop over the low lava rock wall, and skirt the edge of the golf course along the cliff's edge. Views extend south across the beautiful bay to Puu Olai (Hike 13). From the grassy bluffs, a path heads inland through the picnic area to the second parking lot. Return along the same paths.

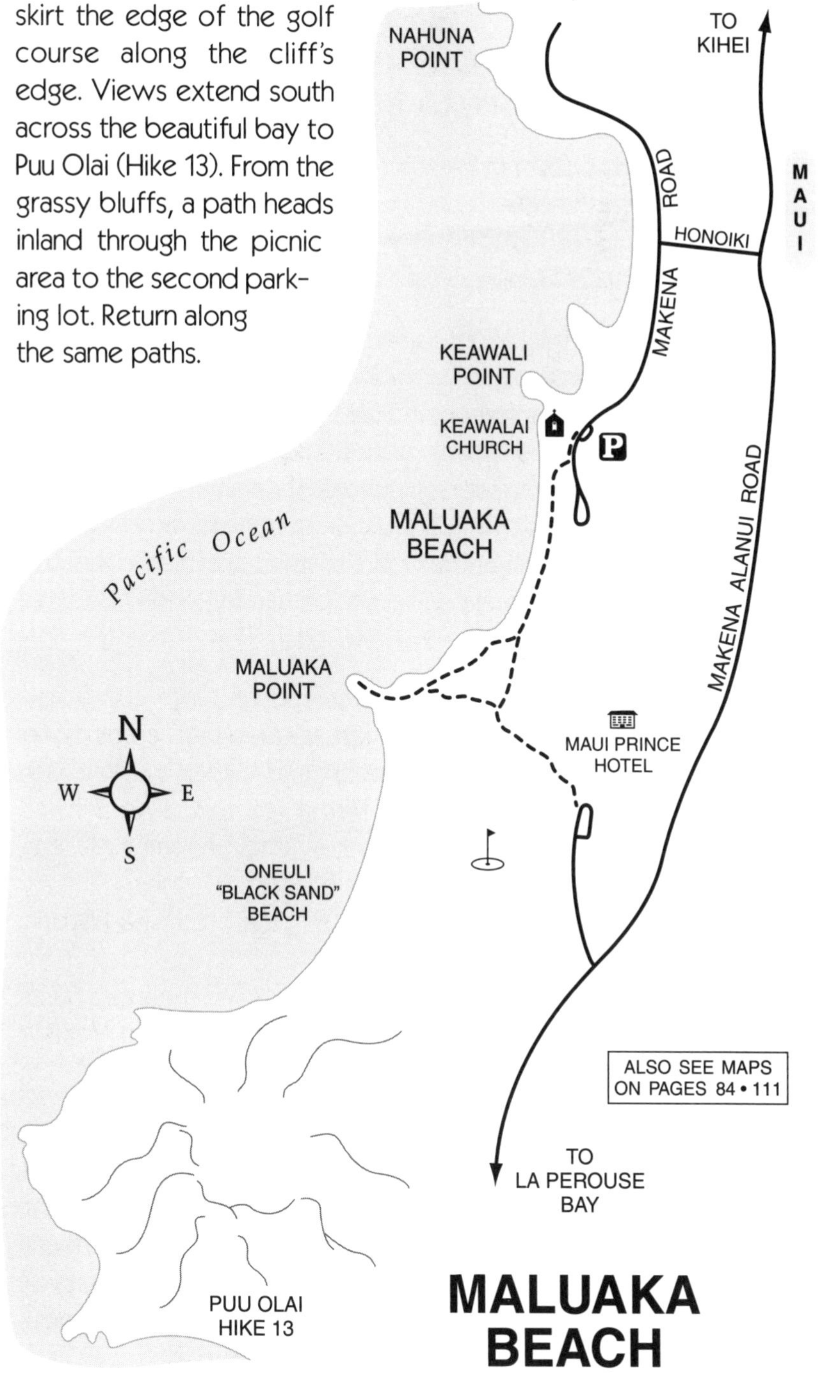

NAHUNA POINT

TO KIHEI

MAKENA ROAD

HONOIKI

MAUI

KEAWALI POINT

KEAWALAI CHURCH

P

MALUAKA BEACH

Pacific Ocean

MALUAKA POINT

MAKENA ALANUI ROAD

N
W        E
S

MAUI PRINCE HOTEL

ONEULI "BLACK SAND" BEACH

ALSO SEE MAPS ON PAGES 84 • 111

TO LA PEROUSE BAY

PUU OLAI HIKE 13

# MALUAKA BEACH

# Hike 13
## Puu Olai "Red Hill"
### FROM ONELOA "MAKENA" BEACH

**Hiking distance:** 1 mile round trip
**Hiking time:** 1 hour
**Elevation gain:** 400 feet
**Maps:** U.S.G.S. Makena

**Summary of hike:** Puu Olai is a 360-foot weathered volcanic tuft that protrudes out to sea at the south end of Wailea. The dormant cinder cone separates Oneloa "Makena" Beach from Oneuli "Black Sand" Beach. At the base of the Puu Olai are lava formations and tidepools, dividing Makena Beach into Big Beach and Little Beach (an unofficial clothing optional beach). This hike begins on Big Beach and follows the long and wide crescent of sand to the base of the cinder cone. The trail explores the tidepools fronting Puu Olai, then climbs the volcanic slope to panoramic views across the ocean to the islands of Lanai, Molokini, and Kahoolawe.

**Driving directions:** At the south end of Kihei, the South Kihei Road ends. The road curves left at the signed entrance to Wailea on Okolani Drive. Go one block to the junction with Wailea Alanui Road on the right. Turn right and drive 4.8 miles south to the signed Makena State Beach turnoff. (Wailea Alanui Road becomes Makena Alanui Road along the way.) Turn right on the entrance road, and park in the lot a short distance ahead.

**Hiking directions:** Walk out to the wide crescent of white sand along Big Beach. Follow the wide strand to the right. Head about 200 yards northwest to the base of Puu Olai, the hill separating Big Beach from Little Beach. Climb up the low lava wall to the ridge overlooking the two beaches. Begin ascending the steep trail to the right on the southern slope of Puu Olai. There are magnificent vistas at the summit. After savoring the views, return to the base of the hill, and venture out on the lava point, where tidepools abound. Explore along your own route.

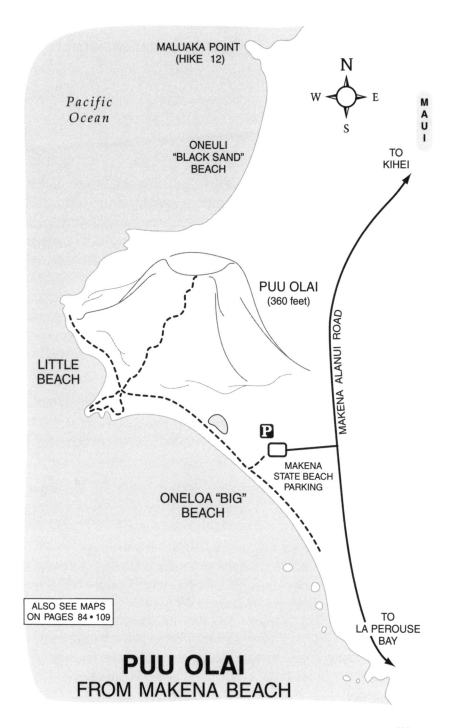

MALUAKA POINT
(HIKE 12)

*Pacific Ocean*

ONEULI
"BLACK SAND"
BEACH

N

W E

S

MAUI

TO
KIHEI

PUU OLAI
(360 feet)

MAKENA ALANUI ROAD

LITTLE
BEACH

P

MAKENA
STATE BEACH
PARKING

ONELOA "BIG"
BEACH

ALSO SEE MAPS
ON PAGES 84 • 109

TO
LA PEROUSE
BAY

# PUU OLAI
## FROM MAKENA BEACH

# Hike 14
## La Perouse Bay to Cape Hanamanioa

**Hiking distance:** 3 miles round trip
**Hiking time:** 1.5 hours
**Elevation gain:** 50 feet
**Maps:** U.S.G.S. Makena

**Summary of hike:** This hike begins at La Perouse Bay, an isolated bay at the southwest tip of Maui. The trail passes tidepools, rocky coves, lava formations, ancient rock walls, and enclosures to a light beacon on the tip of Cape Hanamanioa. The oceans surrounds the beacon on three sides while Haleakala towers above to the northeast. The hike skirts La Perouse Bay along a rutted jeep road that runs parallel to the "King's Highway." The "King's Highway," an ancient Hoapili Trail, was constructed with rough lava rock between 1824—1840.

**Driving directions:** At the south end of Kihei, the South Kihei Road ends. The road curves left at the signed entrance to Wailea on Okolani Drive. Go one block to the junction with Wailea Alanui Road on the right. Turn right and drive 7.8 miles south, passing Wailea and Makena, to the end of the paved road. The signed parking area is on the left side of the road. (Wailea Alanui Road becomes Makena Alanui Road.)

**Hiking directions:** Head south on the unpaved road, parallel to the ocean. The road joins the shoreline and curves around La Perouse Bay. Under the shade of kiave trees, pass tidepools and lava formations. At 0.5 miles, just beyond Beau Chien Beach, the sandy, shaded trail crosses a stark lava field. On the right is an ancient square lava rock enclosure. On the left, at the fenceline, is an signed connector path to the Hoapili "King's Highway" Trail. Continue on the jeep road, passing a second connector trail with the Hoapili Trail at one mile. Follow the rutted road up the hill onto Cape Hanamanioa to a saddle overlooking La Perouse Bay. The extensive lava flow on the slope of Haleakala can be seen from here. The loose, rocky trail makes walking difficult. Continue 0.3 miles to the southwest point of Cape Hanamanioa at the light beacon surrounded by ocean. Narrow side paths lead to several overlooks; fisherman trails follow the low sea cliffs. Return by taking the same path back.

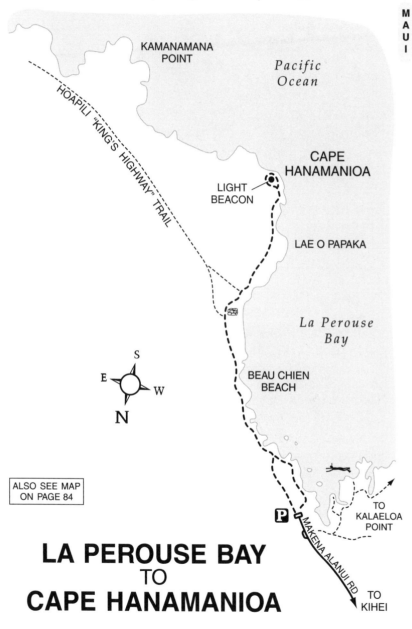

MAUI

KAMANAMANA POINT

*Pacific Ocean*

HŌAPILI "KING'S HIGHWAY" TRAIL

CAPE HANAMANIOA

LIGHT BEACON

LAE O PAPAKA

*La Perouse Bay*

S
E O W
N

BEAU CHIEN BEACH

ALSO SEE MAP ON PAGE 84

P

TO KALAELOA POINT

MAKENA ALANUI RD

TO KIHEI

# LA PEROUSE BAY
## TO
# CAPE HANAMANIOA

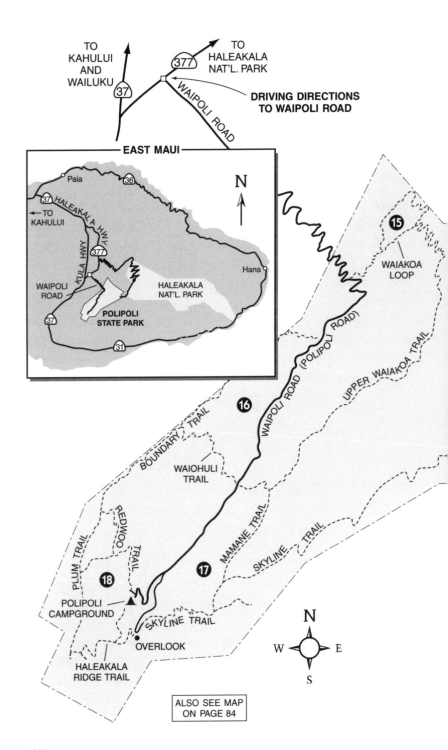

# POLIPOLI STATE PARK
# KULA FOREST RESERVE

M
A
U
I

Polipoli State Park, at 6,200 feet, is part of the 12,000-acre Kula Forest Reserve on the upper southern and western slopes of Haleakala. An extensive trail system crisscrosses the highland forest reserve and connects to the summit of Haleakala. Well-marked trails weave through a profusion of giant redwoods, Monterey cypress, sugi pine, cedar, eucalyptus, plum, alder, and ash groves introduced in the 1920s and 1930s. The quiet, exotic, cloud-shrouded forest, with an understory of ferns and mosses, is reminiscent of the Pacific Northwest. The paths lead to old ranger stations, Civilian Conservation Corps (CCC) bunkhouses, cinder cones, caves, and a campground. Panoramic views extend across Central and West Maui, including the islands of Lanai, Molokai, and Kahoolawe.

TO
HALEAKALA
NAT'L. PARK

The weather is frequently damp and cool due to the high altitude. Wear appropriate clothing.

## Driving directions to Waipoli Road:

From Kahului, near the airport, head east on the Hana Highway (36), and turn right on the Haleakala Highway (37). Drive 14 miles upcountry, passing Pukalani, to the second signed junction with 377, just before mile marker 14. (Highway 37 becomes the Kula Highway after Pukalani.) Turn left onto 377 (Kekaulike Avenue). Continue 0.4 miles to Waipoli Road and turn right.

Continue down Waipoli Road in accordance with each hike's directions.

# Hike 15
# Waiakoa Loop Trail
## POLIPOLI STATE PARK

**Hiking distance:** 4.5 miles round trip
**Hiking time:** 2 hours
**Elevation gain:** 600 feet
**Maps:** U.S.G.S. Kilohana
      Recreational Trails of the Kula Forest Reserve

**Summary of hike:** The Waiakoa Loop is a 3-mile loop trail in the Kula Forest Reserve on the slopes of Haleakala. The hike contours the hillside with panoramic views down country and across open grasslands. Switchbacks then descend 500 feet into a draw, winding through forested groves of eucalyptus and pines. The hike connects with the trail system inside Polipoli State Park.

**Driving direction:** Follow the driving directions on page 115 to Waipoli Road. From Waipoli Road, continue 5 miles up this steep winding road to the signed Waiakoa Trail on the left by the green hunter check-in station. Park on the left off the road.

**Hiking directions:** Head north past the hunter station on the dirt road overlooking the valley. Cross Kaonoulu Gulch and enter a eucalyptus forest, reaching the Kula Forest Reserve trailhead sign and gate at 0.75 miles. A short distance past the gate is a trail split and the start of the loop. Take the footpath uphill to the right and cross Naalae Gulch. Emerge from the trees to fantastic views on the open rolling grasslands. The path reaches a signed junction with the Upper Waiakoa Trail at 1.3 miles. This route bears to the right, connecting with the Mamane and Waihuli Trails (Hike 17). Continue straight, traversing the hillside and crossing Keahuaiwi Gulch. Curve left, descending 500 feet on five switchbacks into the shaded pine forest. Curve left again and return to the south. Switchbacks steadily wind back up the hillside, completing the loop. Bear to the right, retracing your steps to the parking area.

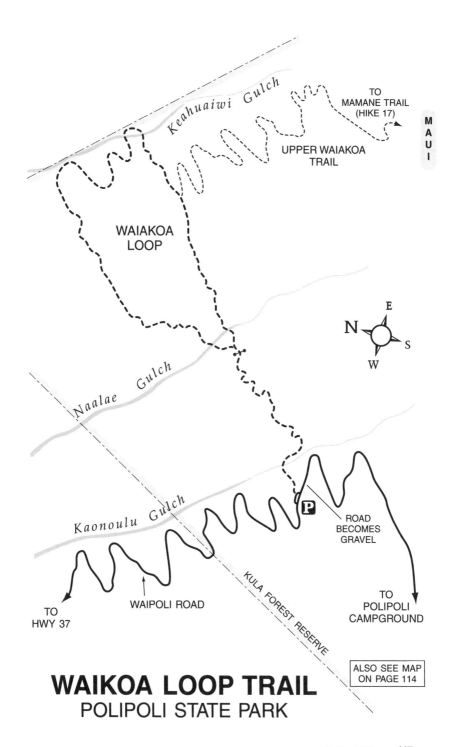

TO MAMANE TRAIL (HIKE 17)

*Keahuaiwi Gulch*

UPPER WAIAKOA TRAIL

MAUI

WAIAKOA LOOP

*Naalae Gulch*

N E S W

*Kaonoulu Gulch*

P

ROAD BECOMES GRAVEL

KULA FOREST RESERVE

WAIPOLI ROAD

TO HWY 37

TO POLIPOLI CAMPGROUND

ALSO SEE MAP ON PAGE 114

# WAIKOA LOOP TRAIL
## POLIPOLI STATE PARK

# Hike 16
# Boundary—Waiohuli Loop
## POLIPOLI STATE PARK

**Hiking distance:** 5.8 mile loop
**Hiking time:** 3 hours
**Elevation gain:** 850 feet
**Maps:** U.S.G.S. Kilohana and Lualailua Hills
Recreation Trails of the Kula Forest Reserve

**Summary of hike:** The Boundary-Waiohuli Loop winds through the shade of a towering forest with a lush understory of vegetation. The forested path descends along the north Kula Forest Reserve boundary, then follows the west boundary to an old cabin at the junction with the Waiohuli Trail. The Waiohuli Trail climbs 800 feet, passing through dense stands of redwood, cedar, and ash trees.

**Driving directions:** Follow the driving directions on page 115 to Waipoli Road. From Waipoli Road, continue 5.9 miles up this steep winding road to the end of the pavement. Follow the unpaved road a half mile to the signed Boundary Trail on the right. Park on the side of the road.

**Hiking directions:** Take the Boundary Trail and immediately descend into the dense forest to the west. The path weaves a half mile downhill to the northwest boundary of the Kula Forest Reserve. Curve south, skirting the west boundary through the deep forest. Cross numerous small gulches. At 2.6 miles, the trail reaches a signed junction by a rustic shelter on the left. The right fork continues on the Boundary Trail towards the old ranger station at the Redwood Trail junction. Leave the Boundary Trail, and take the Waiohuli Trail to the left. Steadily climb through the dense forest, reaching the Waipoli Road at 4 miles. Follow the forested access road to the left for 1.8 miles, completing the loop at the trailhead.

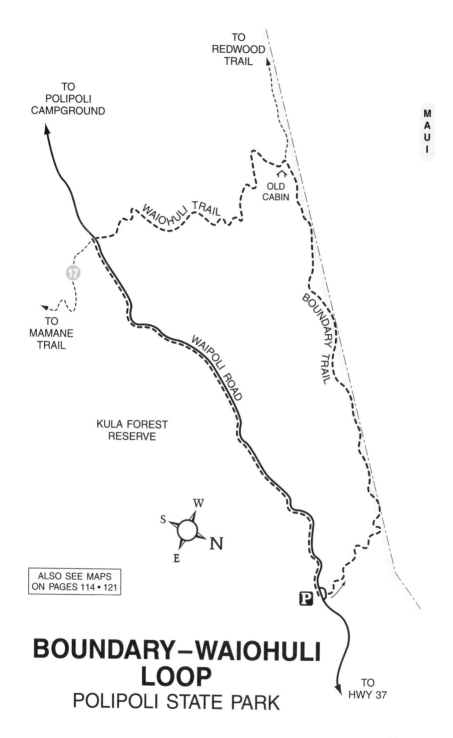

TO REDWOOD TRAIL

TO POLIPOLI CAMPGROUND

OLD CABIN

WAIOHULI TRAIL

M A U I

⑰

TO MAMANE TRAIL

BOUNDARY TRAIL

WAIPOLI ROAD

KULA FOREST RESERVE

W
S — N
E

ALSO SEE MAPS ON PAGES 114 • 121

P

TO HWY 37

# BOUNDARY–WAIOHULI
# LOOP
## POLIPOLI STATE PARK

# Hike 17
## Mamane—Skyline Loop
### POLIPOLI STATE PARK

**Hiking distance:** 4 mile loop
**Hiking time:** 2 hours
**Elevation gain:** 850 feet
**Maps:** U.S.G.S. Lualailua Hills and Makena
        Recreation Trails of the Kula Forest Reserve

**Summary of hike:** The Mamane Trail leads to a small volcanic cone and cave shelter before joining the Skyline Trail at 7,300 feet. The Skyline Trail is a dirt road that follows the ridge along the southwest slope of Haleakala all the way to Science City Road near the Haleakala summit. This hike follows the lower portion of the trail, looping back through Polipoli State Park.

**Driving directions:** Follow the driving directions on page 115 to Waipoli Road. From Waipoli Road, continue 5.9 miles up this steep winding road to the end of the pavement. Follow the unpaved road 2.3 miles to the signed Waiohuli Trail on both sides of the road. Park on the side of the road.

**Hiking directions:** Take the signed Waiohuli Trail on the left (east) side of the road, heading uphill. Zigzag up the mountain through a pine forest, reaching a signed junction at 0.7 miles. The left fork leads to the Waiakoa Loop Trail (Hike 30) on the Upper Waiakoa Loop. Take the right fork on the Mamane Trail. There are caves and a lava pit crater on the right. Wind steadily up the mountain, reaching Skyline Trail, an unpaved road, at 1.9 miles. Bear to the right on the dirt road, and descend along the exposed slope through a eucalyptus grove for a half mile to a trail junction. Again bear right, winding down the mountain to a sharp hairpin bend in the road. On the bend is an overlook and a junction with the Haleakala Ridge Trail. Follow the road downhill, passing the junction with the campground road on the left. Continue straight ahead on the Waipoli Road one mile, completing the loop back at the trailhead.

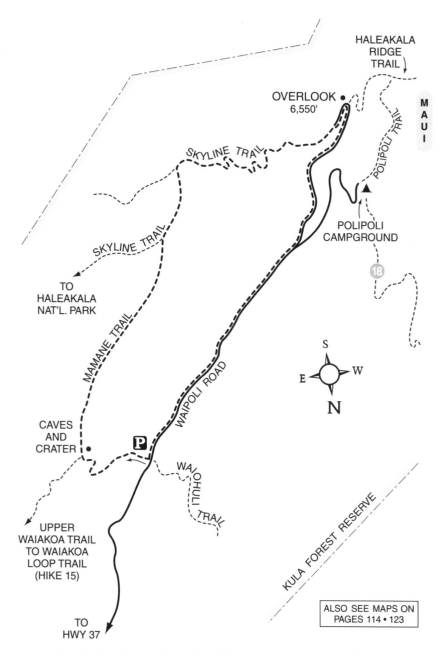

HALEAKALA RIDGE TRAIL

OVERLOOK ●
6,550'

M A U I

SKYLINE TRAIL

POLIPOLI TRAIL

POLIPOLI CAMPGROUND

SKYLINE TRAIL

18

TO HALEAKALA NAT'L. PARK

MAMANE TRAIL

WAIPOLI ROAD

S
E ⊕ W
N

CAVES AND CRATER ●

P

WAIOHULI TRAIL

UPPER WAIAKOA TRAIL TO WAIAKOA LOOP TRAIL (HIKE 15)

KULA FOREST RESERVE

TO HWY 37

ALSO SEE MAPS ON PAGES 114 • 123

# MAMANE–SKYLINE LOOP
## POLIPOLI STATE PARK

# Hike 18
# Polipoli Loop
## POLIPOLI STATE PARK

**Hiking distance:** 4.9 mile loop
**Hiking time:** 2.5 hours
**Elevation gain:** 1,000 feet
**Maps:** U.S.G.S. Lualailua Hills and Makena
Recreation Trails of the Kula Forest Reserve

**Summary of hike:** The Polipoli Loop is a combination of four forested trails. The hike begins at the picnic area and campground on the Polipoli Trail and connects with the Haleakala Ridge Trail. A side path near the junction with the Plum Trail leads to a cinder cone containing a small shelter cave. The Plum Trail gently winds through redwood, ash, and sugi pine groves, often shrouded in an atmospheric mist. On the return leg of the loop is an old ranger station by a huge wall of flowering hydrangea bushes.

**Driving directions:** Follow the driving directions on page 115 to Waipoli Road. From Waipoli Road, continue 5.9 miles up this steep winding road to the end of the pavement. Follow the unpaved road 3.3 miles to a road split. Take the right fork 0.6 miles, descending to the campground and parking area at the end of the road.

**Hiking directions:** Facing the campground, take the signed Polipoli Trail on the right. Head south in the cedar, cypress, and pine forest to a T-junction with the Haleakala Ridge Trail at 0.6 miles. Take the right fork, winding downhill through eucalyptus, mahogany, and cypress around the west side of Polipoli Peak. At the junction, bear left for a short detour to the cinder cone and cave. Return to the junction and continue downhill to the end of the trail at 1.5 miles. Take the Plum Trail to the right (north) on a gentle grade along the contours of the mountain-side. At 2.6 miles is a signed junction. The Tie Trail on the right returns back to Polipoli Park for a four-mile loop. Stay to the left, descending to the ranger station and the Redwood Trail junction 0.6 miles ahead. Begin ascending the mountain. Pass the CCC bunkhouse on the right and the Tie Trail junction, reaching a camping cabin near the campground. Bear left on the dirt road to the campground access road, and head back to the campground.

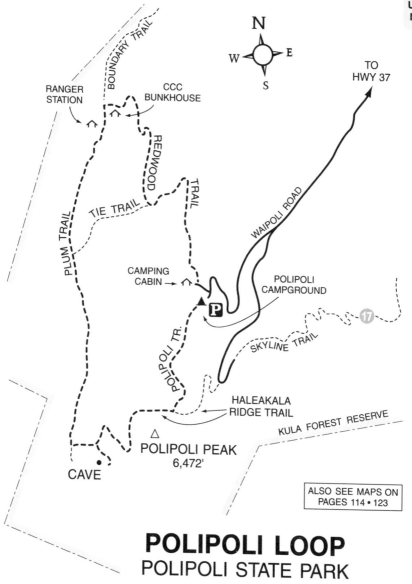

**POLIPOLI LOOP**
POLIPOLI STATE PARK

ALSO SEE MAPS ON
PAGES 114 • 123

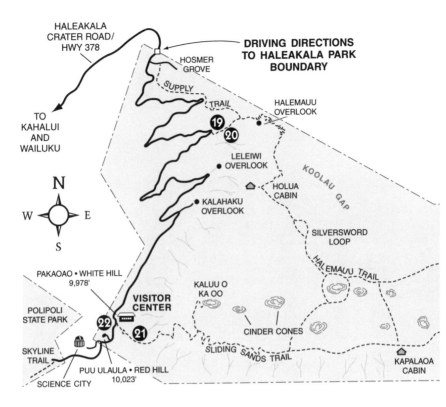

Haleakala is the world's largest dormant volcano. Its expansive crater stretches seven miles long, 2.5 miles wide, and 3,000 feet deep. Twenty-seven thousand acres were designated as Haleakala Crater National Park to preserve its unique features. The twisting park road follows along the crater's west rim, the highest elevation on Maui. From the crater, the park extends east down the Kipahulu Valley to the ocean at Oheo Gulch south of Hana. A string of multi-colored cinder cones, lava flows, and fields of volcanic ash line the surreal crater floor with 36 miles of interconnected, well-marked trails. Hikes 19—22 explore some of these trails, from the volcanic foothills to the 10,023-foot summit, and from the magnificent crater rim to the stark, lunar landscape of the crater floor. The trails lead to cinder cones, lava caves, panoramic overlooks, and a camping cabin. Be sure to pack warm clothes, as the temperatures are much cooler at this 10,000-foot elevation.

# HALEAKALA CRATER
## NATIONAL PARK

M
A
U
I

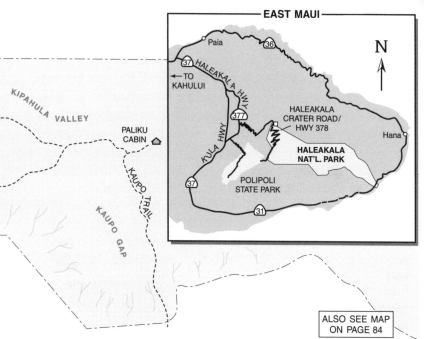

Driving directions to Haleakala park boundary: From the junction of the Haleakala Highway (37) and the Hana Highway (36) near the airport, take the Haleakala Highway (37) upcountry. Head southeast 7.7 miles, a half mile past Pukalani, to the first junction with Highway 377. Turn left on Highway 377 (the Haleakala Highway), continuing uphill to a junction with Highway 378/Haleakala Crater Road. Turn left and zigzag up the mountain to the Haleakala park boundary.

Continue from the park boundary in accordance with each hike's directions.

# Hike 19
# Halemauu Trail to Crater Rim Overlook
## HALEAKALA NATIONAL PARK

**Hiking distance:** 1.5 miles round trip
**Hiking time:** 45 minutes
**Elevation gain:** 250 feet
**Maps:** U.S.G.S. Kilohana
　　　　Trails Illustrated Haleakala National Park

**Summary of hike:** The Halemauu Trail descends from the west rim of the Haleakala Crater and crosses the crater floor to the eastern end. This hike follows the first mile of the trail, traversing the upper slope across the alpine scrubland to an overlook at the edge of the crater. From the rim are expansive views of the northern flanks of Haleakala, Koolau Gap, and the moist cliffs of Leleiwi. The crater floor is dotted with several multi-colored cinder cones.

**Driving directions:** From the Haleakala park boundary, continue 4.5 miles to the trailhead turnoff on a sharp hairpin bend in the road, between mile markers 14 and 15. Turn left into the trailhead parking lot.

**Hiking directions:** Head southeast past the information sign and curve left towards the rim. Gradually descend along the slopes of Haleakala across the alpine shrubland. At 0.6 miles, pass the junction with the Supply Trail, a pack route from Hosmer Grove that intersects from the left. Continue down the easy descent on the rocky path to a trail gate. Pass through the gate and zigzag down a short distance to the rim of the crater and overlook. This is our turnaround spot.

To hike further, continue with Hike 20. The switchbacks steeply descend over 1,000 feet along the crater wall. Follow the crater floor, reaching Holua Cabin at 3.9 miles from the trailhead.

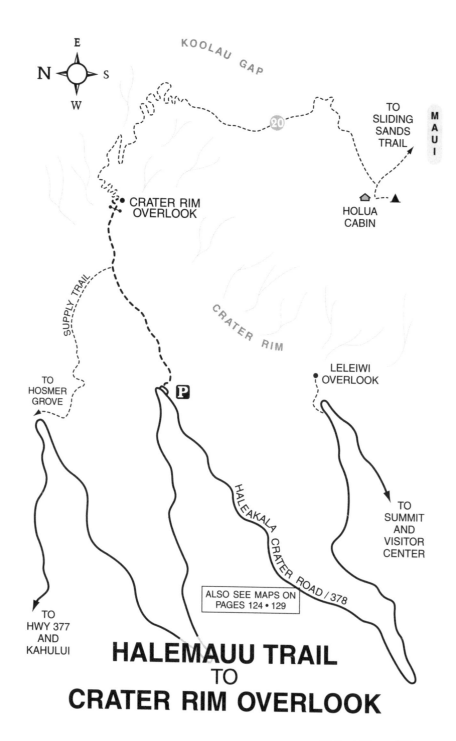

KOOLAU GAP

N E S W

20

TO SLIDING SANDS TRAIL

M A U I

CRATER RIM OVERLOOK

HOLUA CABIN

SUPPLY TRAIL

CRATER RIM

TO HOSMER GROVE

LELEIWI OVERLOOK

P

TO SUMMIT AND VISITOR CENTER

HALEAKALA CRATER ROAD / 378

ALSO SEE MAPS ON PAGES 124 • 129

TO HWY 377 AND KAHULUI

# HALEMAUU TRAIL
## TO
# CRATER RIM OVERLOOK

# Hike 20
# Halemauu Trail to Holua Cabin
## HALEAKALA NATIONAL PARK

**Hiking distance:** 7.8 miles round trip
**Hiking time:** 4 hour
**Elevation gain:** 1,400 feet
**Maps:** U.S.G.S. Kilohana
       Trails Illustrated Haleakala National Park

**Summary of hike:** The Halemauu Trail to Holua Cabin descends the sheer cliffs of Haleakala on the west crater wall. The trail begins at 8,000 feet, where dramatic switchbacks zigzag down to Koolau Gap on the crater floor. Along the way are magnificent views into the crater and down the Keanae Valley to the ocean. On the cliffs behind the cabin is a cave; a hundred yards to the east is a lava tube. This hike can be combined with the Sliding Sands Trail (Hike 21) for a one-way 11.5-mile shuttle hike.

**Driving directions:** From the Haleakala park boundary, continue 4.5 miles to the trailhead turnoff on a sharp hairpin bend in the road, between mile markers 14 and 15. Turn left into the trailhead parking lot.

**Hiking directions:** Follow the hiking directions from Hike 19 to the overlook at the rim of the crater. From the overlook, begin the awesome descent, snaking down the narrow ridge on steep switchbacks. The moonscape views inside the crater are magnificent. At the crater floor by Koolau Gap is a trail gate. Pass through the gate and follow the floor along the base of the crater wall through a grassy meadow. At 3.9 miles, the trail reaches a signed junction by Holua Cabin, sitting above the trail on a lava plateau. This is our turnaround spot. The right fork leads to the cabin on a grassy flat near the crater wall. A short distance to the south of the cabin is a campground.

From the junction, the Halemauu Trail continues to a junction with the Sliding Sands Trail and on to the east end of the crater.

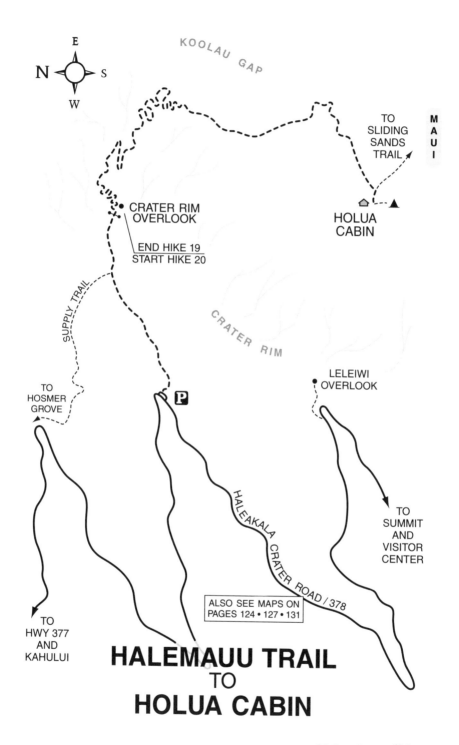

N
E
S
W

KOOLAU GAP

TO SLIDING SANDS TRAIL

M A U I

CRATER RIM OVERLOOK

END HIKE 19
START HIKE 20

HOLUA CABIN

SUPPLY TRAIL

CRATER RIM

TO HOSMER GROVE

LELEIWI OVERLOOK

P

TO SUMMIT AND VISITOR CENTER

HALEAKALA CRATER ROAD / 378

ALSO SEE MAPS ON PAGES 124 • 127 • 131

TO HWY 377 AND KAHULUI

# HALEMAUU TRAIL
## TO
# HOLUA CABIN

# Hike 21
## Sliding Sands Trail to Kaluu o Ka Oo
### HALEAKALA NATIONAL PARK

**Hiking distance:** 5 miles round trip
**Hiking time:** 3 hours
**Elevation gain:** 1,600 feet
**Maps:** U.S.G.S. Kilohana
Trails Illustrated Haleakala National Park

**Summary of hike:** Kaluu o Ka Oo is a multi-colored cinder cone on the south end of the Haleakala Crater. The cinder cone is below the ridge of Red Hill near the summit of Haleakala. The Sliding Sands Trail, located by the visitor center, descends into the crater on a cinder and ash path. The trail follows the base of the south rim into the barren moonscape with continuous magnificent vistas. A half-mile spur trail climbs to the rim of Kaluu o Ka Oo, offering views into the cinder cone.

**Driving directions:** From the Haleakala park boundary, continue 10.5 miles to the visitor center parking lot on the left, near the summit of Haleakala.

**Hiking directions:** Circle around to the right (south) side of Pakaoao (White Hill), and parallel the road for a short distance to the rim of the crater. You will see Kaluu o Ka Oo (the first cinder cone below), and the Sliding Sands Trail disappearing into the stark vastness. Begin the steady descent on a few switchbacks into the immense crater along the south wall. At just under a mile, pass a distinct rock formation with flowering shrubs. Curve right, away from the outcropping. Continue down to a signed junction at two miles by lava formations near the crater floor. Leave the Sliding Sands Trail and bear left (north). Descend steeply, then the path levels out and traverses the hillside towards the cinder cone. Pass numerous silversword plants and begin the short ascent to the edge of the colorful cone. Look into the depression from atop Kaluu o Ka Oo. A rough trail circles the rim.

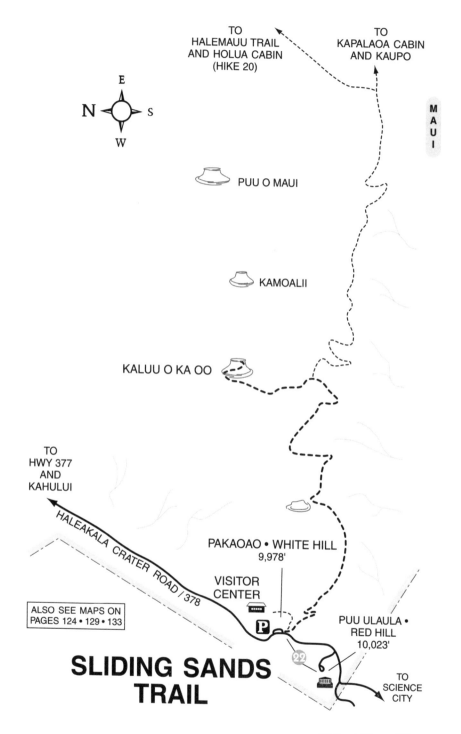

TO
HALEMAUU TRAIL
AND HOLUA CABIN
(HIKE 20)

TO
KAPALAOA CABIN
AND KAUPO

M
A
U
I

N E S W

PUU O MAUI

KAMOALII

KALUU O KA OO

TO
HWY 377
AND
KAHULUI

HALEAKALA CRATER ROAD / 378

PAKAOAO • WHITE HILL
9,978'

VISITOR
CENTER

ALSO SEE MAPS ON
PAGES 124 • 129 • 133

P

22

PUU ULAULA •
RED HILL
10,023'

TO
SCIENCE
CITY

# SLIDING SANDS
# TRAIL

# Hike 22
# Pakaoao (White Hill) and Puu Ulaula (Red Hill)
## HALEAKALA NATIONAL PARK

**Hiking distance:** 0.7 miles round trip
**Hiking time:** 1 hour
**Elevation gain:** 150 feet
**Maps:** U.S.G.S. Kilohana
Trails Illustrated Haleakala National Park

**Summary of hike:** Pakaoao (White Hill) is the favorite spot for experiencing the world-renowned Haleakala sunrise. White Hill is adjacent to the visitor center, with a book store and exhibits about the volcano. The awesome views from the 9,778 hilltop extend into and across the immense crater.

Puu Ulaula (Red Hill) is a cinder cone on the southwest rim of Haleakala. At 10,023 feet, the hill is the highest spot on Maui. The vistas take in the entire island of Maui, the offshore islands of Lanai, Molokai, Kahoolawe, and the Big Island to the southeast. A 360-degree glass-enclosed observation and exhibit building allows for weather-sheltered panoramic views.

**Driving directions:** From the Haleakala park boundary, continue 10.5 miles to the visitor center parking lot on the left near the summit of Haleakala.

Puu Ulaula Overlook is 0.5 miles past the visitor center at the enclosed observation shelter on Maui's highest point. Park in the lot by the shelter.

**Hiking directions:** The White Hill hike begins at the visitor center. The short quarter-mile trail loops to the right (south). Curve around the basaltic knob on the gentle grade, gaining 150 feet up to the summit. The path nearly forms a loop. From the overlook, Sliding Sands Trail (Hike 21) can be seen disappearing into the vast crater.

The Red Hill stroll circles the parking area from the summit of Maui. The paths take you to numerous vista overlooks and the glass-enclosed viewing shelter. Meander along your own route.

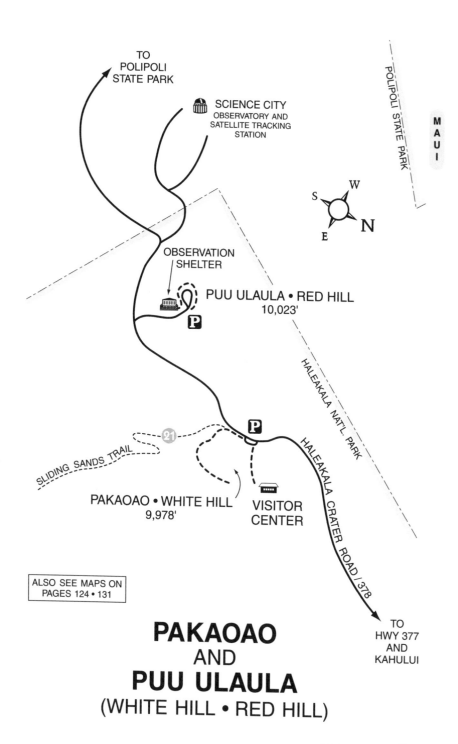

TO
POLIPOLI
STATE PARK

SCIENCE CITY
OBSERVATORY AND
SATELLITE TRACKING
STATION

POLIPOLI STATE PARK

MAUI

W
S
N
E

OBSERVATION
SHELTER

P

PUU ULAULA • RED HILL
10,023'

HALEAKALA NATL. PARK

P

SLIDING SANDS TRAIL

21

PAKAOAO • WHITE HILL
9,978'

VISITOR
CENTER

HALEAKALA CRATER ROAD / 378

ALSO SEE MAPS ON
PAGES 124 • 131

TO
HWY 377
AND
KAHULUI

# PAKAOAO
## AND
# PUU ULAULA
### (WHITE HILL • RED HILL)

# Hike 23
## Waihou Spring Trail
### WAIHOO SPRING FOREST RESERVE

**Hiking distance:** 2.4 miles round trip
**Hiking time:** 1.5 hours
**Elevation gain:** 400 feet
**Maps:** U.S.G.S. Kilohana
Maui Recreation Map

**Summary of hike:** Waihou Spring Trail is above the up-country town of Makawao in the Waihou Spring Forest Reserve. The beautiful reserve borders the state-run tree experimentation project planted in the 1920s. The trail begins on the tree plantation road and loops through a forest of Monterey cypress, pines, eucalypti, and koa. A side path leads to an overlook and descends into Kailua Gulch at an enclosed, boulder-strewn canyon with numerous caves. Old water diversion tunnels are cut into the face of the surrounding cliffs.

**Driving directions:** From Hana Highway (36) in downtown Paia, take Baldwin Avenue 7 miles upcountry to Makawao Avenue in the town of Makawao. Continue straight through the intersection—Baldwin Avenue changes to Olinda Road. Drive 4.9 miles up the winding road to the Waihou Spring trailhead on the right by the signed Tree Growth Research Area entrance, located 0.9 miles past mile marker 11.

**Hiking directions:** Walk past the signed gate, and take the unpaved road south into the pine forest. The soft trail, covered in pine needles, borders the tree experimentation project on the left. At 0.2 miles, as the road curves left, leave the road and take the signed trail to the right. Continue under the shade of a dense forest canopy to a junction at 0.4 miles. Begin the loop to the right to a signed junction with the spur trail to the overlook and spring. Bear right on the narrow footpath, and head gently downhill a quarter-mile to an overlook with a bench. Switchbacks lead down the hillside to the rock-enclosed forested canyon. Numerous caves are in the surrounding cliffs. The spring is dry but the location is fascinating to explore. Return up the mountain past the overlook and back to the loop trail. Go to the right, meandering through the open forest and completing the loop. Return to the right.

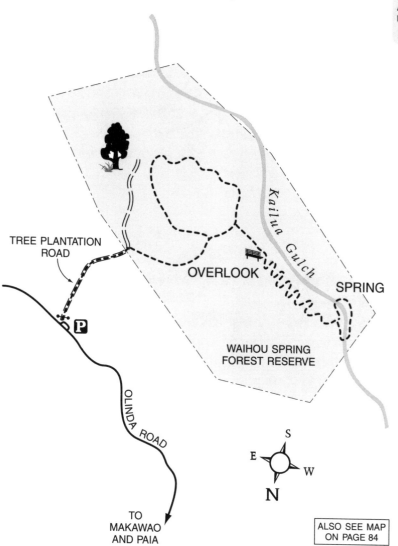

TREE PLANTATION
ROAD

OVERLOOK

*Kailua Gulch*

SPRING

P

WAIHOU SPRING
FOREST RESERVE

OLINDA ROAD

S
E ✧ W
N

TO
MAKAWAO
AND PAIA

ALSO SEE MAP
ON PAGE 84

# WAIHOO SPRING

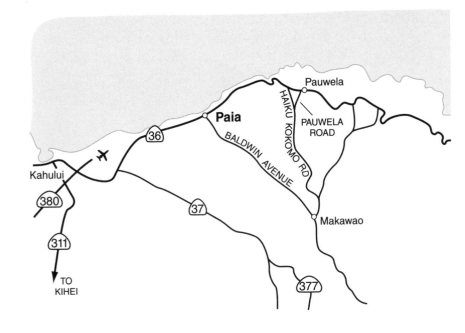

## HIKES 24–30
# THE HANA HIGHWAY

The Hana Highway is a gorgeous, winding 55-mile road that traverses the northeast slopes of Haleakala along the edge of the windward coastal cliffs. Along the way are magnificent waterfalls, freshwater swimming pools, diverse beaches, moist lowland forests, lush rainforests, deep stream-fed canyons, steep valleys, breathtaking seascape vistas, state and county parks, and more than fifty one-lane bridges. This is among the most scenic drives in Hawaii and the world. The drive is a slow trek with many magnificent places to stop, hike, swim, and explore, easily making the trip a full day's experience. It is advisable not to rush by spending a night or two in Hana.

Hikes 24—58 are on the road to Hana, and Hikes 29 and 30 are at Ohea Gulch, a short distance past the town of Hana. From Paia, Hana is 44 miles—driving directions and mileages originate from Paia.

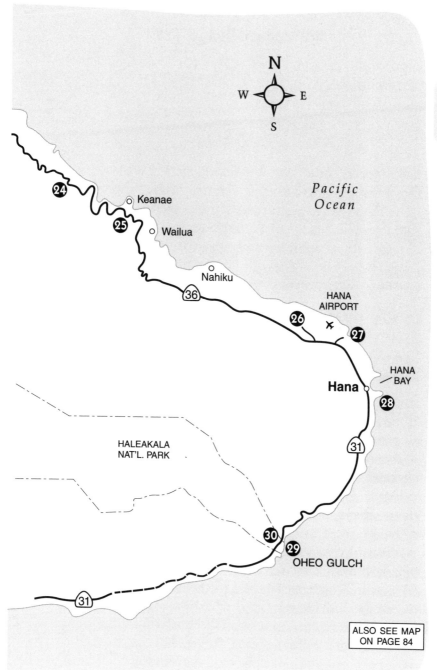

N
W · E
S

MAUI

24

○ Keanae

25

○ Wailua

*Pacific Ocean*

○ Nahiku

36

HANA AIRPORT

26

27

**Hana** ○

HANA BAY

28

HALEAKALA NAT'L. PARK

31

30

29

OHEO GULCH

31

ALSO SEE MAP ON PAGE 84

# Hike 24
# Waikamoi Ridge Trail

**Hiking distance:** 1.2 miles round trip
**Hiking time:** 30 minutes
**Elevation gain:** 200 feet
**Maps:** U.S.G.S. Keanae
   Island of Maui Recreation Map

**Summary of hike:** The Waikamoi Ridge Trail is an interpretive nature trail in a tropical forest. The trail climbs the dense vegetated slope to a grassy clearing and sheltered picnic area, offering great views of Keanae Peninsula and the ocean. A mosaic of tree roots crosses the trail through the lush rain forest that is adorned with groves of bamboo, paperback eucalypti, mahogany, heliconia, philodendrons, and ginger.

**Driving directions:** From the junction of Hana Highway (36) and Baldwin Avenue in downtown Paia, take the Hana Highway 19.2 miles to the signed trailhead parking area on the right, between mile markers 9 and 10.

**Hiking directions:** Walk up the paved ramp past the trail sign to the first picnic area in a stand of large eucalyptus trees. Take the path to the left, and descend through the lush forest for a short distance. Climb up the hillside to a bench at an overlook of a deep gorge, Waikamoi Stream, and the Hana Highway. Continue up the steps, following the ridge to a junction. The right fork returns to the trailhead. Take the left fork uphill to a second trail split. Curve left and continue following the ridge. At a half mile the path ends on a grassy hilltop clearing at a sheltered picnic area and bamboo forest. Return on the same path back to the trail split. Take the route that is now on your left, heading downhill to the picnic area near the trailhead. Bear left, curving down to the parking area.

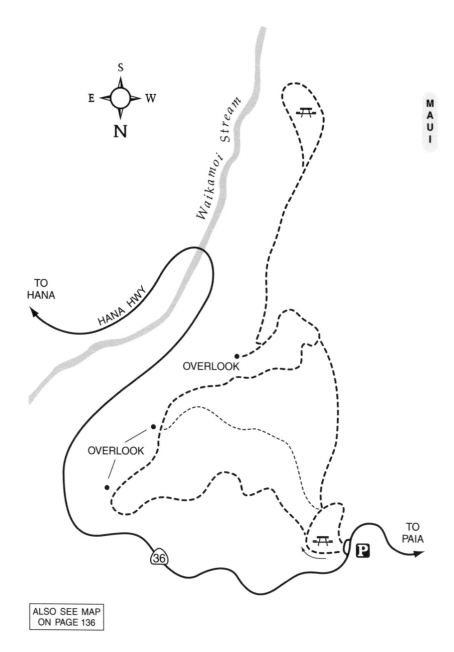

# WAIKAMOI RIDGE TRAIL

# Hike 25
# Keanae Arboretum

**Hiking distance:** 1.6 miles round trip
**Hiking time:** 1 hour
**Elevation gain:** Level
**Maps:** U.S.G.S. Keanae
       Island of Maui Recreation Map

**Summary of hike:** The Keanae Arboretum is a six-acre oasis with a profusion of flowering and fruit-bearing plants. The arboretum is divided into three sections—native forest trees, introduced tropical trees, and cultivated Hawaiian plants. Piinaau Stream cascades from the rainforest through the lush arboretum, forming several swimming holes.

**Driving directions:** From the junction of Hana Highway (36) and Baldwin Avenue in downtown Paia, take the Hana Highway 26.3 miles to the parking pullouts on the right by the signed arboretum gates. The pullouts are located in a shady hairpin turn between mile markers 16 and 17.

**Hiking directions:** Pass the green gate and follow the jeep road 0.2 miles along Piinaau Stream to the signed Keanae Arboretum entrance gate. Inside the arboretum, the paved path parallels Piinaau Stream through an open grassy area with introduced fruit and ornamental trees. Short side paths lead down to the stream and pools. Continue along the unpaved path lined with ti plants. Pass through the Hawaiian cultivated plant section with irrigated taro patches between lava rock walls. There are banana, sweet potato, sugar cane, ginger, and papaya plants. The rocky path skirts the taro patches to the south arboretum boundary at a half mile.

To hike further, the muddy path narrows and is usually slippery. Cross Pokakaekane Stream, leave the banks of Piinaau Stream, and follow Kuo Stream through the rain forest. The trail frequently crosses the stream, passing small pools. Choose your own turnaround spot.

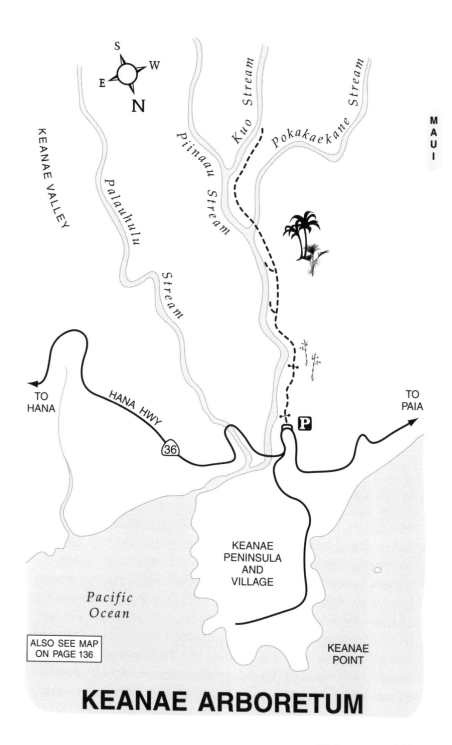

S / W / E / N

MAUI

KEANAE VALLEY

Palauhulu

Stream

Piinau Stream

Kuo Stream

Pokakaekane Stream

TO
HANA

HANA HWY

36

P

TO
PAIA

KEANAE
PENINSULA
AND
VILLAGE

Pacific
Ocean

ALSO SEE MAP
ON PAGE 136

KEANAE
POINT

# KEANAE ARBORETUM

# Hike 26
# Ulaino Road Trail
# to Blue Pool and Blue Angel Falls

**Hiking distance:** 4 miles round trip
**Hiking time:** 2 hours
**Elevation gain:** 120 feet
**Maps:** U.S.G.S. Hana
 Island of Maui Recreation Map

**Summary of hike:** Blue Angel Falls cascades 100 feet off the fern-covered lava cliffs into Blue Pool on the beach a few steps from the ocean. The hike down Ulaino Road passes through a lush tropical forest with kukui, hala, and guava trees. The road ends at a cove by the abandoned village of Ulaino, where old stone walls overtaken by the jungle still remain. Heleleikeoha Stream flows through the rocky cove, forming a shallow lagoon before entering the sea.

**Driving directions:** From the junction of Hana Highway (36) and Baldwin Avenue in downtown Paia, take the Hana Highway 43.5 miles to the signed Ulaino Road. Turn left and drive 0.7 miles to the end of the paved road. Park alongside the road.

From Hana, drive 3 miles northwest on the Hana Highway to the Ulaino Road turnoff, located one mile past the signed Waianapanapa State Park turnoff.

**Hiking directions:** Follow the road northwest under the forest canopy. At a half mile, cross Honomaele Stream by Kahanu Gardens on the right. Continue through the forest, passing a few homesteads on each side of the road. Stay on the main road, disregarding smaller road forks. The trail ends near the mouth of Heleleikeoha Stream, where the stream empties into the ocean 100 yards to your right. Shortly before Heleleikeoha Stream, the remains of Ulaino village are on the right, which are gradually being overtaken by the jungle vegetation. Wade across the stream and follow the coastline west a few hundred yards along the cobblestone beach. Blue Angel

Falls and Blue Pool, a large swimming hole at the base of the waterfall, will be on the left. Return along the same path.

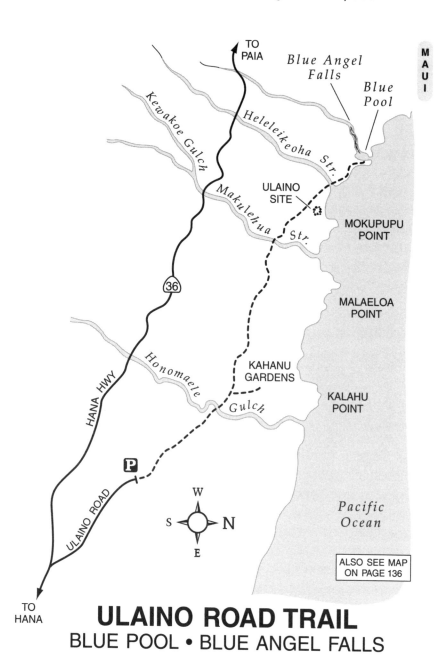

**ULAINO ROAD TRAIL**
BLUE POOL • BLUE ANGEL FALLS

# Hike 27
# Hana—Waianapanapa Coastal Trail
## WAIANAPANAPA STATE PARK

**Hiking distance:** 4.5 miles round trip
**Hiking time:** 2.5 hours
**Elevation gain:** Nearly level
**Maps:** U.S.G.S. Hana
       Island of Maui Recreation Map

**Summary of hike:** The Hana-Waianapanapa Trail follows a portion of the ancient "Kings Highway" from Pailoa Bay in Waianapanapa State Park to Kainalimu Bay in a shady heliotrope grove northwest of Hana Bay. The hike follows the jagged, windswept coastal cliffs, crossing lava flows above caves, underground tunnels, and irregular islets. The trail passes blowholes, sea arches, tidepools, and an ancient Hawaiian temple site. Smooth hand-set stepping stones are still in place along the aa lava and cinder path.

**Driving directions:** From Hana, drive 2 miles northwest on the Hana Highway to the signed Waianapanapa State Park turnoff, just before mile marker 32. Turn right and drive a half mile down the forest road to the state park. Turn left and go 0.2 miles to the parking lot.

From Baldwin Avenue in downtown Paia, take the Hana Highway 44.5 miles to the signed Waianapanapa State Park turnoff and turn left. Follow the directions above.

**Hiking directions:** Take the paved path to the right through a tree grove to a trail split. The left fork descends to Black Sand Beach (Hike 47). Follow the right fork across the basalt bluffs above Pailoa Bay to a second junction. The left fork follows the contours of the rugged coastline and rejoins the main trail a short distance ahead. Continue past jagged lava formations and arches jutting out to sea. Cross a natural bridge over a turbulent ocean inlet. At 0.8 miles the path reaches the lava rock walls of Ohala Heiau, a good turnaround spot for a shorter hike.

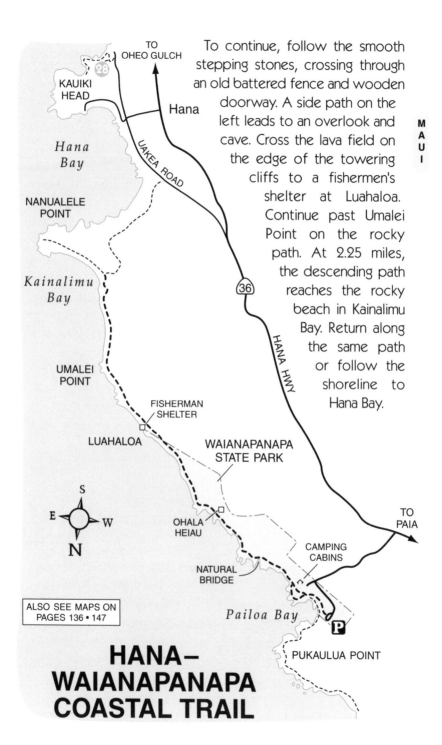

TO
OHEO GULCH

28

KAUIKI
HEAD

Hana

UAKEA ROAD

M
A
U
I

*Hana
Bay*

NANUALELE
POINT

*Kainalimu
Bay*

36

HANA HWY

UMALEI
POINT

FISHERMAN
SHELTER

LUAHALOA

WAIANAPANAPA
STATE PARK

S
E ⊕ W
N

OHALA
HEIAU

TO
PAIA

CAMPING
CABINS

NATURAL
BRIDGE

ALSO SEE MAPS ON
PAGES 136 • 147

*Pailoa Bay*

P

PUKAULUA POINT

# HANA–
# WAIANAPANAPA
# COASTAL TRAIL

To continue, follow the smooth stepping stones, crossing through an old battered fence and wooden doorway. A side path on the left leads to an overlook and cave. Cross the lava field on the edge of the towering cliffs to a fishermen's shelter at Luahaloa. Continue past Umalei Point on the rocky path. At 2.25 miles, the descending path reaches the rocky beach in Kainalimu Bay. Return along the same path or follow the shoreline to Hana Bay.

# Hike 28
# Kaihalulu "Red Sand" Beach

**Hiking distance:** 1 mile round trip
**Hiking time:** 1 hour
**Elevation gain:** 50 feet
**Maps:** U.S.G.S. Hana

**Summary of hike:** Kaihalulu "Red Sand" Beach is a hidden gem in the town of Hana on the isolated south side of Kauiki Head. The secluded, clothing-optional beach is set in a small pocket cove enclosed by towering volcanic cliffs. The red sand originates from the eroded volcanic cinders spilling off the cliffs. The exotic looking beach is often protected from the strong ocean currents by a large, jagged lava rock barrier that forms a natural sea wall. The only access to the beach is from a narrow, eroded cliff-hugging trail above the ocean.

**Driving directions:** From the town of Hana, take Uakea Road (by Hana Bay) 0.3 miles to the end of the road at the south end of Kauiki Head. Park along the side of the road.

**Hiking directions:** Facing the ocean, on the left side of the Hotel Hana Maui, cross the open field on the left towards Kauiki Head. Take the well-worn footpath, and curve towards the ocean to a trail split by a large ironwood tree. To the left is a Japanese cemetery. Take the right fork and descend on the short, steep path to the edge of the ocean cliffs. Bear left, below the cemetery, on the narrow path along the eroded cliffs. Use good judgement and caution as the footing is challenging due to loose cinders. A few dips and rises on the cliff shelf leads to the northeast point of Kaihalulu Bay. Curve around the point into the naturally carved amphitheater at Red Sand Beach. Descend the cliffs along the south end of the cove into the protected sandy beach pocket.

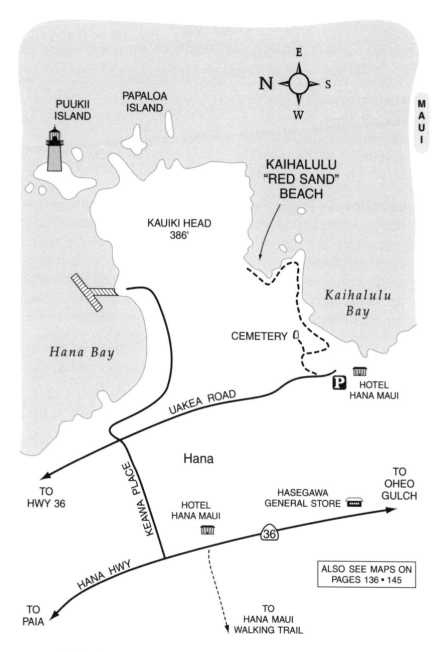

# KAIHALULU "RED SAND" BEACH

# Hike 29
# Seven Sacred Pools
## OHEO GULCH

**Hiking distance:** 0.6 mile loop
**Hiking time:** 1 hour
**Elevation gain:** 100 feet
**Maps:** U.S.G.S. Kipahulu
        Trails Illustrated Haleakala National Park

**Summary of hike:** Oheo Gulch, commonly known as Seven Sacred Pools, has a succession of natural staircase waterfalls cascading into a series of descending pools. The pools, numbering far more than seven, are bordered by sculpted lava rock basins and cliffs which lie along Oheo Gulch above the rugged eastern coastline at Kuloa Point. This short hike includes swimming holes and hikes around a series of freshwater pools that overlook the black lava rock oceanfront. Oheo Gulch is preserved as part of Haleakala National Park.

The twisting, winding road from Hana to the pools weaves along the coastline through valleys and ridges. The scenic drive passes waterfalls and crosses numerous one-lane bridges.

**Driving directions:** From Hana, drive 7 miles south on Highway 36, which becomes Highway 31 after Hana, to the signed parking lot past mile marker 42. It is on the ocean side of the road by the Kipahulu Ranger Station and visitor center.

**Hiking directions:** Follow the clearly marked path towards the visitor center and ocean. Cross the grassy slope and picnic area to the bluffs overlooking the ocean. On the right are rock wall remnants of an ancient Hawaiian village. Curve left, reaching the stream in Oheo Gulch by a series of five large swimming pools and numerous smaller pools, which are all connected by cascades and small waterfalls. Follow the succession of pools up the south side of Oheo Stream. At the bridge, a footpath returns to the parking lot.

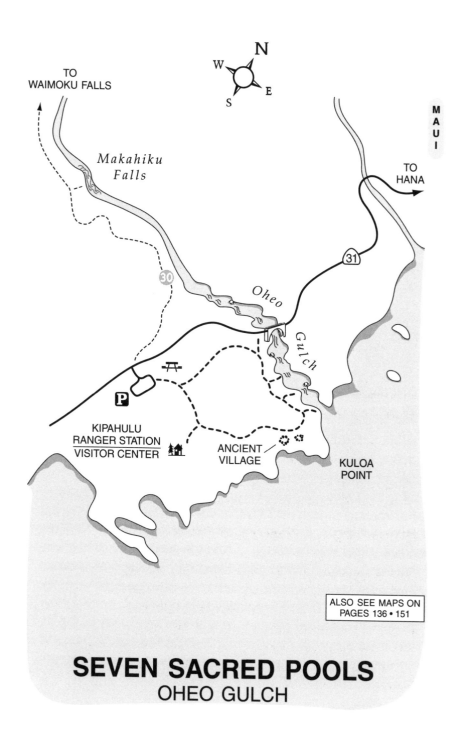

TO
WAIMOKU FALLS

N
W          E
S

*Makahiku
Falls*

*Oheo*

*Gulch*

MAUI

TO
HANA

31

30

P

KIPAHULU
RANGER STATION
VISITOR CENTER

ANCIENT
VILLAGE

KULOA
POINT

ALSO SEE MAPS ON
PAGES 136 • 151

# SEVEN SACRED POOLS
## OHEO GULCH

# Hike 30
## Pipiwai Trail to
## Makahiku and Waimoku Falls

**Hiking distance:** 4 miles round trip
**Hiking time:** 2 hours
**Elevation gain:** 800 feet
**Maps:** U.S.G.S. Kipahulu
Trails Illustrated Haleakala National Park

**Summary of hike:** Makahiku Falls and Waimoku Falls are towering cataracts on the streams above Oheo Gulch (Hike 29). Makahiku Falls, a half mile from the trailhead, plunges 185 feet off the forested cliff into the deep gorge. The trail ends further up the stream at the base of Waimoku Falls, set in a 400-foot rock wall amphitheater. The hike parallels Oheo Stream and Pipiwai Stream up the wet verdant valley, passing ancient taro farm sites and crossing two bridges. The jungle includes guava, mango, Christmas-berry trees, and towering bamboo forests.

**Driving directions:** Follow the driving directions from Hike 29 to the Kipahulu Ranger Station and visitor center.

**Hiking directions:** The Pipiwai Trail begins on the inland side of the Hana Highway, across the road from the ranger station parking lot. Begin climbing up the pastureland along the left side of Oheo Gulch. At a half mile, a side path on the right leads to the forested Makahiku Falls cliffside overlook. Return to the main trail and continue uphill through the rain forest. At just under a mile, cross a bridge over Oheo Stream below the confluence of Palikea Stream and Pipiwai Stream, which form Oheo Stream. A short distance ahead, cross a second bridge over Pipiwai Stream. Enter the first of three cool and dark bamboo forests. Boardwalks aid in crossing the muddy areas. Just past the third bamboo forest, cross several channels of Pipiwai Stream to the shallow pool in front of Waimoku Falls. The waterfall free-falls off the mossy, fern-covered cliffs into the pool. Return on the same path.

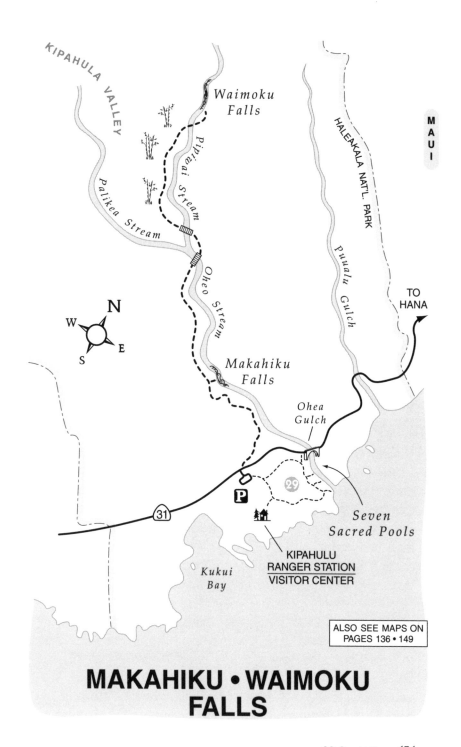

KIPAHULA VALLEY

*Waimoku Falls*

*Pipiwai Stream*

*Palikea Stream*

*Oheo Stream*

HALEAKALA NATL. PARK

*Puualu Gulch*

M A U I

TO HANA

N
W   E
S

*Makahiku Falls*

*Ohea Gulch*

31

P

29

*Seven Sacred Pools*

*Kukui Bay*

KIPAHULU
RANGER STATION
VISITOR CENTER

ALSO SEE MAPS ON
PAGES 136 • 149

# MAKAHIKU • WAIMOKU FALLS

# Oahu

PAGES 153–219

# Island of Oahu

A hike along the coast or into the backcountry will most certainly enhance your time spent on this tropical island. These 30 hikes take you to the island's best trails. The entire coastline is included as well as scenic high-country hikes in the Koolau Mountains. All levels of hiking experience are accommodated, from easy beach strolls to mountain climbs that reward the hiker with sweeping views. An overall map of Oahu and the locations of the hikes is found on the next page.

The Hawaiian Islands are among the most beautiful and dramatic tropical landscapes on earth. The islands are 500 miles from any other island and 2,500 miles from the nearest continent. The landscape is covered with verdant green mountains, active and dormant craters, remote canyons, lush flora and fauna, countless waterfalls, colored sand beaches, and coral reefs. Warm, turquoise ocean water surrounds the islands. The temperature hovers around 80 degrees with sunshine and gentle winds. Trade winds buffet the northeast side of each island, creating dense rain forests and exotic tropical plants. The southwest regions have barren desert-like terrain covered with cactus plants. Oahu offers easy access to swimming, snorkeling, diving, windsurfing, boating, fishing, bicycling, sunbathing, people watching, and, of course, hiking.

These hikes offer a variety of lush valleys, spectacular waterfalls, volcanic craters, gardens, tropical swimming holes, coastal beaches, tidepools, ridge trails, and intimate rainforest hikes. Use the hikes' summaries to choose the best hike to match your preferences.

Oahu houses more than 70 percent of the Hawaiian Islands' population and is also the most popular tourist destination. When most people think of Oahu, they imagine the capital city of Honolulu with its world-famous skyline and the white sand beaches of Waikiki. Diamond Head, a 760-foot crater at the west end of Waikiki, has sweeping views of the city from its summit. (Hike 4 leads into the crater and up to its summit.)

Oahu has much more to offer, however, than Honolulu and the beaches of Waikiki. The many hiking trails which take you away from the crowds showcase the island's natural beauty. The cliffs and craters of the southeast point are explored in Hikes 1—3. The Koolau Mountains, only two miles north of Waikiki, contain a network of hiking trails in the rain forest and along mountain ridges and valleys (Hikes 5—12). The views from atop the Pali Lookout (Hike 13) are incredible. Hikes 14—22 include deep tropical forests, gardens, and waterfalls.

The east coast of Oahu has a variety of sandy beaches and jagged, steep mountains. The charming, small communities of Kailua and Kaneohe can be visited on the way to the coastal hikes along the windward coast (Hikes 27—30). Kahana Valley, inland from the town of Kahana, is a 5,000-acre forest with picnic areas, hiking trails, and cultural shrines (Hikes 29 and 30).

Take time to visit the north shore and leeward coast, where there is one beautiful beach after another. This area is known for its great surfing and the world-class waves of the Banzai Pipeline, Sunset Beach, and Waimea Bay. The Waianae Mountains and 4,000-foot Mount Kaala dominate the landscape behind these beaches. The leeward coast includes undisturbed tide-pools, sandy coves, and jungle valleys. The Kaunala Trail (Hike 26), a favorite hike, leads through a jungle up to a ridgeop vista of the leeward coast. Hikes 23 and 24 on Kaena Point, the westernmost peninsula of Oahu, includes tidepools, sea caves, arches, blowholes, dunes, and a crashing surf along the volcanic coastline.

Be sure to bring hats, sunscreen, insect repellent, sunglasses, snacks, and drinking water. The trails can be (and usually are) slippery due to rain and mud. Use caution and wear shoes with traction. Bring swimsuits and outdoor gear to use at the coast.

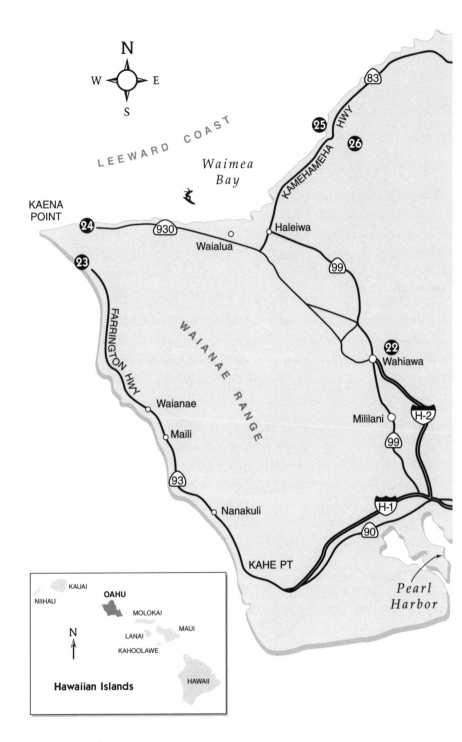

N
W E
S

LEEWARD COAST

*Waimea Bay*

KAENA POINT

83
25
26

KAMEHAMEHA HWY

24
930
Haleiwa
Waialua
23
99

FARRINGTON HWY

WAIANAE RANGE

22 Wahiawa

Waianae
Mililani
H-2

Maili
99

93
H-1

Nanakuli
90

KAHE PT

*Pearl Harbor*

KAUAI
NIIHAU
OAHU
MOLOKAI
N
LANAI
MAUI
KAHOOLAWE
HAWAII

Hawaiian Islands

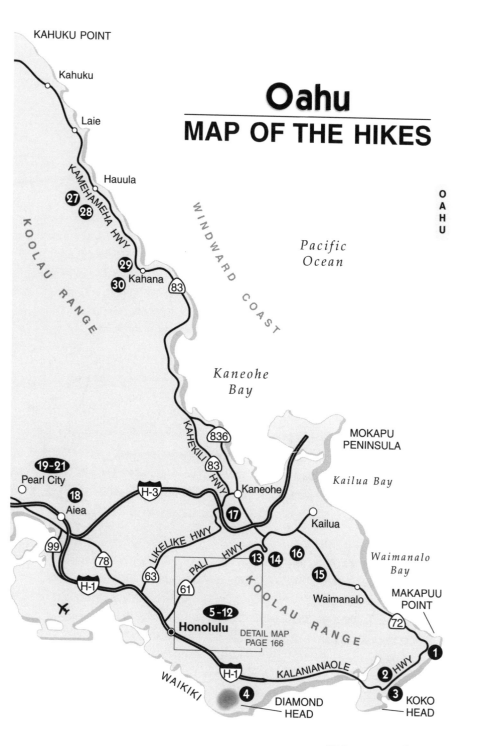

# Oahu
## MAP OF THE HIKES

KAHUKU POINT

Kahuku

Laie

Hauula

KAMEHAMEHA HWY

KOOLAU RANGE

WINDWARD COAST

*Pacific Ocean*

OAHU

27
28
29
30 Kahana
83

*Kaneohe Bay*

KAHEKILI HWY

836
83

MOKAPU PENINSULA

*Kailua Bay*

19-21
Pearl City

18
Aiea

H-3

99

78

H-1

63

LIKELIKE HWY

PALI HWY

61

5-12
**Honolulu**

DETAIL MAP
PAGE 166

Kaneohe

17

13 14 16

Kailua

15

*Waimanalo Bay*

Waimanalo

MAKAPUU POINT

72

KOOLAU RANGE

1

2 HWY

3 KOKO HEAD

WAIKIKI

H-1

KALANIANAOLE

4

DIAMOND HEAD

# Hike 1
# Makapuu State Wayside

**Hiking distance:** 2 miles round trip
**Hiking time:** 1.25 hour
**Elevation gain:** 550 feet
**Maps:** U.S.G.S. Koko Head
  Oahu Reference Maps: Honolulu/Oahu South Shore

**Summary of hike:** Makapuu State Wayside sits on the east-ernmost tip of Oahu. This trail, a former lighthouse access road, leads to majestic vistas on Makapuu Point. From the 600-foot ocean bluff are two observation decks, World War II bunkers, and a working lighthouse. Off the shore from the steep cliffs are Manana "Rabbit" Island, an old volcanic crater, and Kaohikaipu "Turtle" Island, both state seabird sanctuaries. Makapuu Point is also an excellent whale watching site.

**Driving directions:** From McCully Street and King Street in Waikiki, go east on King Street one mile. Curve left and enter H-1 east. Continue 12.8 miles to the trailhead pullout. It is locat-ed 4.1 miles beyond the Hanauma Bay turnoff. (Along the way, H-1 becomes the Lunalilo Freeway, which becomes the Kalanianaole Highway/72.) As the highway gains elevation toward the saddle between Makapuu Head and the rest of Oahu, you will see a narrow, paved walking trail head off to the right. Park alongside the road.

**Hiking directions:** Walk up the paved and gated road, steadily heading uphill towards Makapuu Head. The trail passes through two gates and lichen-covered boulders along the way. Koko Crater and Koko Head are prominent in the southwest. As the trail joins the cliff's edge at Puu o Kipahulu, curve left and head north, parallel to the eroded cliffs overlooking the coast-line. As the trail levels out, curve left toward the bunkers at the summit. To the right are the two observation platforms. The lighthouse is 100 feet below near Makapuu Point. After mar-veling at the panoramic vistas, return along the same route

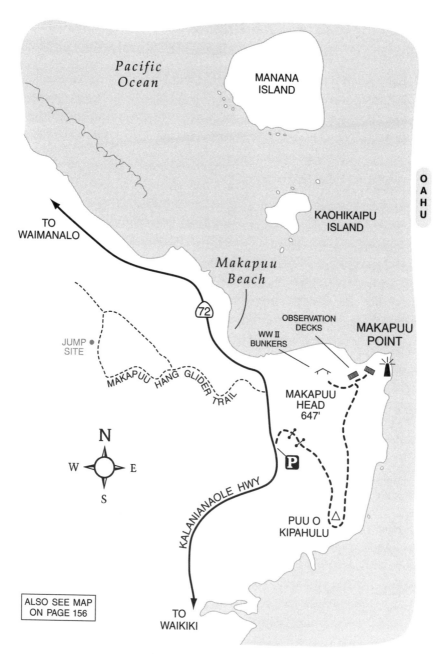

*Pacific Ocean*

MANANA ISLAND

OAHU

KAOHIKAIPU ISLAND

TO WAIMANALO

*Makapuu Beach*

72

JUMP SITE

MAKAPUU HANG GLIDER TRAIL

OBSERVATION DECKS

WW II BUNKERS

MAKAPUU POINT

MAKAPUU HEAD 647'

N
W    E
S

P

KALANIANAOLE HWY

PUU O KIPAHULU

ALSO SEE MAP ON PAGE 156

TO WAIKIKI

# MAKAPUU STATE WAYSIDE

# Hike 2
# Koko Crater Botanic Garden
408 Kealahou Street
Open daily from sunrise to sunset

**Hiking distance:** 2.5 mile loop
**Hiking time:** 1.5 hours
**Elevation gain:** 100 feet
**Maps:** U.S.G.S. Koko Head
Oahu Reference Maps: Honolulu/Oahu South Shore
Koko Crater Botanical Garden map

**Summary of hike:** Koko Crater, historically known as Kohelepelepe, is a dormant, steep-walled cinder cone near the east end of Oahu. Inside the 200-acre crater is a 60-acre botanic garden, still in the early stages of development. The trail loops through the garden around the perimeter of the crater basin. The garden cultivates rare dryland plants, endangered native flora, and includes plants from the Americas, Africa, and Madagascar. The blooming groves of plumeria and bougainvillea are diverse and rich with color and fragrance.

**Driving directions:** From McCully Street and King Street in Waikiki, go east on King Street one mile. Curve left and enter H-1 east. Continue 11.2 miles to Kealahou Street. It is located 2.5 miles beyond the Hanauma Bay turnoff. (Along the way, H-1 becomes the Lunalilo Freeway, which becomes the Kalanianaole Highway/72.) Turn left on Kealahou Street, and drive 0.6 miles to the signed turnoff. Turn left and continue 0.4 miles to the botanic garden at the end of the road.

**Hiking directions:** Walk through the entrance gate, and take the path to the right between the plumeria and bougainvillea groves. At a quarter mile is a trail split, beginning the loop. Follow the right fork past a multicolored hibiscus grove and the cacti. At the west end of the crater, in the Hawaiian plant section, is a signed junction. The left fork heads downhill on the Inner Loop. The right fork heads uphill on the Outer Loop. Both of the trails merge further ahead. After the trails rejoin, complete the loop, returning to the trailhead adjacent to the Koko Crater stables.

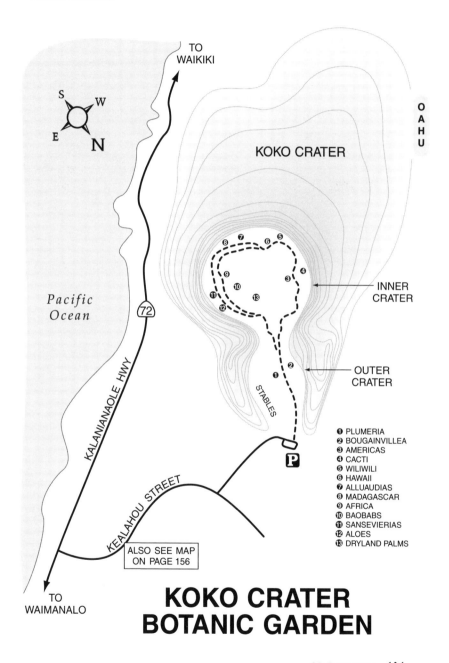

TO WAIKIKI

KOKO CRATER

OAHU

INNER CRATER

OUTER CRATER

Pacific Ocean

72

KALANIANAOLE HWY

STABLES

P

❶ PLUMERIA
❷ BOUGAINVILLEA
❸ AMERICAS
❹ CACTI
❺ WILIWILI
❻ HAWAII
❼ ALLUAUDIAS
❽ MADAGASCAR
❾ AFRICA
❿ BAOBABS
⓫ SANSEVIERIAS
⓬ ALOES
⓭ DRYLAND PALMS

KEALAHOU STREET

ALSO SEE MAP ON PAGE 156

TO WAIMANALO

# KOKO CRATER BOTANIC GARDEN

# Hike 3
# Hanauma Bay to the Toilet Bowl

**Hiking distance:** 1.4 miles round trip
**Hiking time:** 1 hour
**Elevation gain:** 100 feet
**Maps:** U.S.G.S. Koko Head
        Oahu Reference Maps: Central Oahu/Windward Coast

**Summary of hike:** Hanauma Bay is surrounded by volcanic cliffs, palm trees, and a half mile of white sand. The calm, shallow water in the bay make it a popular snorkeling area, abundant with coral reefs and fish. Along the east edge of the bay is a raised terrace. The trail runs along this ledge, passing tidepools and splashing waves to the Toilet Bowl. This natural, 30-foot round hole along the rock terrace fills and empties as the waves wash in and out, resembling a flushing toilet. Hanauma Bay was a filming location for Elvis Presley in *Blue Hawaii* and Burt Lancaster in *From Here To Eternity*.

**Driving directions:** From McCully Street and King Street in Waikiki, go east on King Street one mile. Curve left and enter H-1 east. Continue 8.7 miles to the Hanauma Bay turnoff on the right. (Along the way, H-1 becomes Lunalilo Freeway which becomes Kalanianaole Highway/72.) Turn right and drive 0.3 miles into the parking lot. A parking fee and entrance fee are required.

**Hiking directions:** From the parking lot, pass the entrance station. Descend along a paved walkway to the bay. At the beach, go to the east side (left) of the bay to the raised rock ledge. Follow the rock terrace towards Palea Point. Walk around the first point to the alcove. At the back of this inlet is the Toilet Bowl. Any further, the ocean waves and current become dangerous along the ledge. Return along the same path.

    CAUTION: Unexpected waves splash onto the path. During high tide, it is not advisable to hike here as the waves can sweep you away. Caution signs are posted.

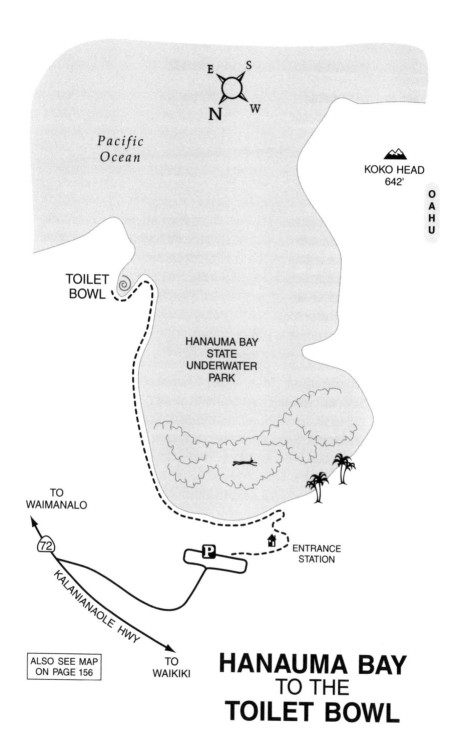

Pacific
Ocean

KOKO HEAD
642'

O A H U

TOILET
BOWL

HANAUMA BAY
STATE
UNDERWATER
PARK

TO
WAIMANALO

ENTRANCE
STATION

(72)

KALANIANAOLE HWY

P

ALSO SEE MAP
ON PAGE 156

TO
WAIKIKI

# HANAUMA BAY
## TO THE
# TOILET BOWL

# Hike 4
# Diamond Head

**Hiking distance:** 1.5 miles round trip
**Hiking time:** 1 hour
**Elevation gain:** 550 feet
**Maps:** U.S.G.S. Honolulu
Oahu Reference Maps: Honolulu/Oahu South Shore

**Summary of hike:** Diamond Head, known to Hawaiians as Leahi, is recognized as Hawaii's most famous landmark. Once used as a military observation station, the dormant volcano is now a state monument. The trail crosses the crater floor and climbs past several scenic overlooks, reaching the 762-foot summit at Point Leahi with postcard-perfect views.  From the bunker atop the summit are incredible 365-degree panoramic vistas of Waikiki, Honolulu, Punchbowl, Koko Head, Koko Crater, the Leeward Coast, and the blue Pacific.

**Driving directions:** From Waikiki, head southeast on Kalakaua Avenue, the main street running through Waikiki. Near the east end, at Kapiolani Park, curve to the left at a road split onto Monsarrat Avenue. Monsarrat Avenue becomes Diamond Head Road. Drive along the north side of the massive crater to the signed Diamond Head State Monument. Turn right. Follow the entrance road through a tunnel to the trailhead parking lot.

**Hiking directions:** Take the paved walkway to the signed trailhead by the restrooms. Head gently uphill along the interior crater floor towards the cliffs at the southwest rim of the cone. The path ascends the crater wall to an overlook of the crater's interior. Climb steps to the entrance of a dark 225-foot tunnel. Walk through the tunnel using the railing as a guide. Once through the tunnel, begin climbing the 99 cement steps, reaching an observation room and a spiral staircase. Wind up the staircase to the World War II bunker at the top. Climb out of the dark bunker to the stunning views of Oahu. To the left are observation platforms at Point Leahi. Return along the same trail.

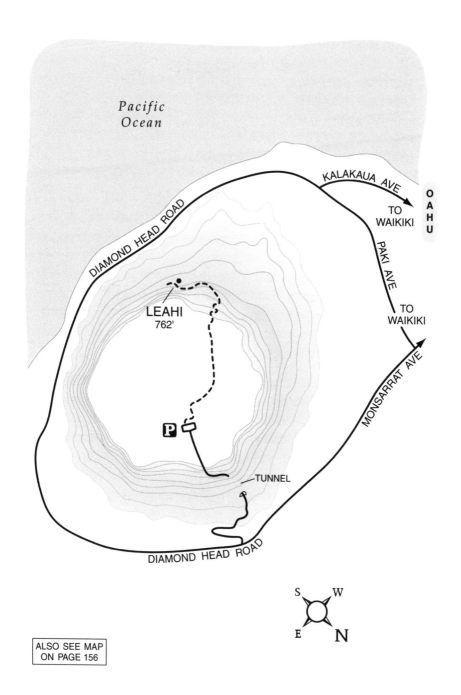

Pacific Ocean

KALAKAUA AVE

OAHU

TO WAIKIKI

DIAMOND HEAD ROAD

PAKI AVE

TO WAIKIKI

LEAHI
762'

MONSARRAT AVE

P

TUNNEL

DIAMOND HEAD ROAD

ALSO SEE MAP
ON PAGE 156

S   W
E   N

# DIAMOND HEAD

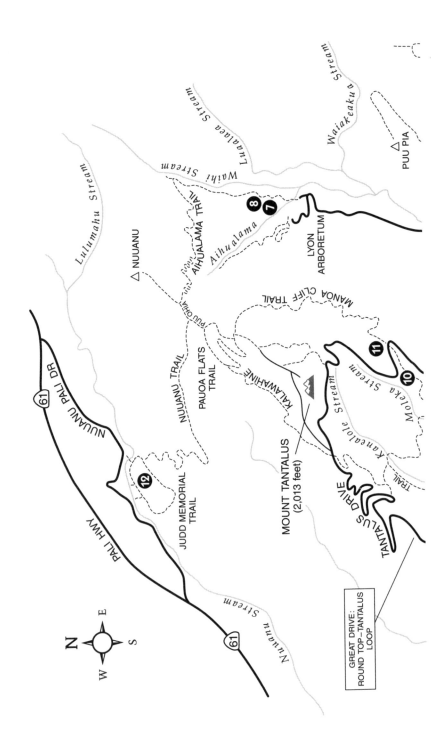

Waiakeakua Stream

Luaalaea Stream

△ PUU PIA

Waihi Stream

Lulumahu Stream

8 7

AIHUALAMA TRAIL

Aihualama

LYON ARBORETUM

△ NUUANU

MANOA CLIFF TRAIL

PUU OHIA TRAIL

NUUANU TRAIL

PAUOA FLATS TRAIL

KALAWAHINE

11

Moleka Stream

10

Kaneaole Stream

MOUNT TANTALUS (2,013 feet)

61

NUUANU PALI DR

12

JUDD MEMORIAL TRAIL

TANTALUS DRIVE

TRAIL

GREAT DRIVE: ROUND TOP-TANTALUS LOOP

PALI HWY

Nuuanu Stream

61

N
E
W    S

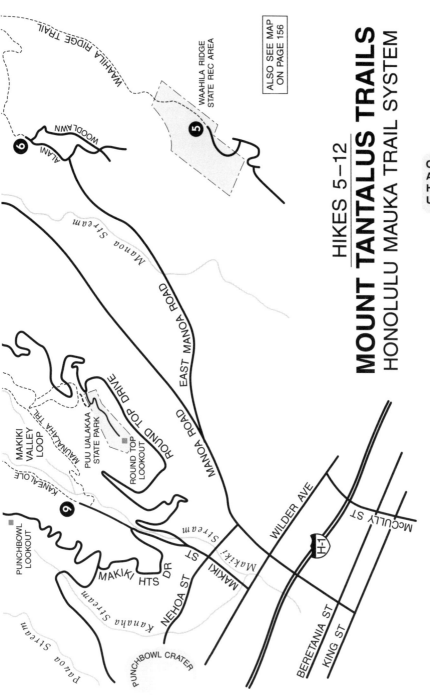

WAAHILA RIDGE TRAIL

WAAHILA RIDGE STATE REC AREA

ALSO SEE MAP ON PAGE 156

WOODLAWN

ALANI

**5**

HIKES 5–12

# MOUNT TANTALUS TRAILS
## HONOLULU MAUKA TRAIL SYSTEM

Manoa Stream

EAST MANOA ROAD

OAHU

MANOA ROAD

ROUND TOP DRIVE

PUU UALAKAA STATE PARK

ROUND TOP LOOKOUT

MAKIKI VALLEY LOOP

MAUNALAHA TRL

KANEALOLE

**6**

PUNCHBOWL LOOKOUT

MAKIKI HTS DR

NEHOA ST

MAKIKI ST

Makiki Stream

WILDER AVE

H-1

BERETANIA ST

KING ST

McCULLY ST

Kanaha Stream

Pauoa Stream

PUNCHBOWL CRATER

# Hike 5
# Waahila Ridge Trail

**Hiking distance:** 3.5 miles round trip
**Hiking time:** 2 hours
**Elevation gain:** 1,000 feet
**Maps:** U.S.G.S. Honolulu
Oahu Reference Maps: Honolulu/Oahu South Shore
Honolulu Mauka Trail System Map

**Summary of hike:** The Waahila Ridge Trail is a forested path the follows the knife-edged spine of this mountain ridge, providing breathtaking panoramas of Manoa Valley, Palolo Valley, Waikiki, and Diamond Head. The ridge route drops and climbs over numerous saddles and knobs, including a few steep and narrow spots. The trail passes through groves of Norfolk Island pine, guava, ironwood, koa, and ohia trees.

**Driving directions:** From Waikiki, take McCully Street to Kapiolani Boulevard. Turn right and drive 1.4 miles to St. Louis Drive. Turn left and follow the winding St Louis Drive 2.3 miles to Bertram Street. Turn right on Bertram Street, and continue a short distance to Peter Street. Turn left on Peter Street, and drive 0.3 miles to Ruth Place. Turn left and enter Waahila Ridge State Recreation Area. The parking lot is 0.3 miles ahead.

**Hiking directions:** Begin at the far end of the parking lot. Several paths pass the picnic tables and continue through Norfolk Island pines. The paths converge and follow the ridge to the first plateau by power poles and a junction at 0.3 miles. Take the right fork downhill, passing many spur trails. Whenever you have a trail choice, stay on the ridge, contouring up and down the spine. The trail reaches a saddle and a junction at 1.7 miles. The wider Kolowalu Trail curves to the left and descends from the head of the valley down a narrow ridge, connecting with the Puu Pia Trail (Hike 6) in the valley below. The right fork follows the ridge to Mt. Olympus but enters the restricted watershed area en route. Return along the same route.

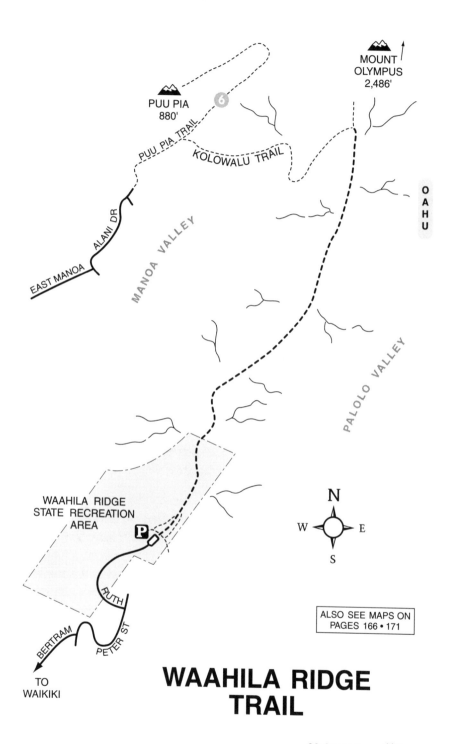

PUU PIA
880'

6

MOUNT
OLYMPUS
2,486'

PUU PIA TRAIL

KOLOWALU TRAIL

ALANI DR

EAST MANOA

MANOA VALLEY

OAHU

PALOLO VALLEY

WAAHILA RIDGE
STATE RECREATION
AREA

P

N
W          E
S

RUTH

BERTRAM

PETER ST

TO
WAIKIKI

ALSO SEE MAPS ON
PAGES 166 • 171

# WAAHILA RIDGE
# TRAIL

# Hike 6
# Puu Pia Trail

**Hiking distance:** 1.8 miles round trip
**Hiking time:** 1 hour
**Elevation gain:** 500 feet
**Maps:** U.S.G.S. Honolulu
Oahu Reference Maps: Honolulu/Oahu South Shore
Honolulu Mauka Trail System map

**Summary of hike:** Puu Pia is an 880-foot mountain that sits in a scenic cirque in Manoa Valley, surrounded by the Honolulu Watershed Forest Reserve. At the summit are sweeping panoramic vistas—from the steep rainforests of the Koolau Range to Waikiki, the blue Pacific, and the volcanic profile of Diamond Head. The trail follows a forested path, climbs the valley to a ridge, and follows the ridge to the summit of Puu Pia.

**Driving directions:** From Waikiki, take McCully Street to Wilder Avenue at the first traffic light after crossing over H-1. Turn left on Wilder Avenue, and drive 0.4 to Punahou Street. Turn right on Punahou Street, which becomes Manoa Road, and drive 0.6 miles to a road split. Take the right fork onto East Manoa Road. Continue 1.8 miles to a T-junction at Alani Drive. Turn left and go 0.2 miles to a junction with Woodland Drive. Park along the side of the road near the junction.

**Hiking directions:** The trail begins as an extension of Alani Drive. Head north on the multi-home driveway at 3689 Alani Drive to the signed trailhead. Enter the jungle path and head uphill 0.2 miles to a trail junction and shelter on a grassy flat. The Kolowalu Trail bears right and climbs a steep narrow ridge, connecting with the Waahila Ridge Trail (Hike 5). Stay left on the Puu Pia Trail, steadily climbing up the damp, shady valley along the right side of a streambed. At 0.6 miles, cross the gully on a horseshoe bend to the left. Steeply climb up the exposed ridge—with awesome views in all directions—to the Puu Pia summit. After savoring the views, return along the same path.

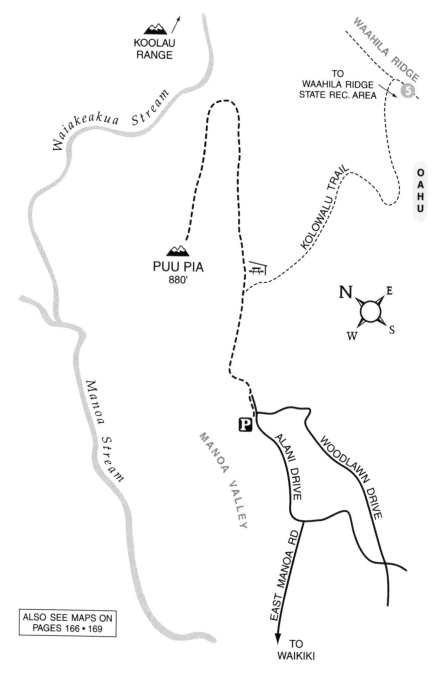

KOOLAU
RANGE

Waiakeakua Stream

TO
WAAHILA RIDGE
STATE REC. AREA

WAAHILA RIDGE

5

OAHU

KOLOWALU TRAIL

PUU PIA
880'

N
E
S
W

Manoa Stream

MANOA VALLEY

P

ALANI DRIVE

WOODLAWN DRIVE

EAST MANOA RD

ALSO SEE MAPS ON
PAGES 166 • 169

TO
WAIKIKI

# PUU PIA TRAIL

# Hike 7
# Manoa Falls

**Hiking distance:** 1.6 miles round trip
**Hiking time:** 1 hour
**Elevation gain:** 500 feet
**Maps:** U.S.G.S. Honolulu
Oahu Reference Maps: Honolulu/Oahu South Shore
Honolulu Mauka Trail System map

**Summary of hike:** Manoa Falls is a towering 100-foot cataract in the beautiful rainforest behind Waikiki. A white ribbon of water cascades off the fern-faced cliffs, fronted by a shallow rock-lined pool. The Manoa Falls Trail parallels Waihi Stream through the forest reserve to the falls. The path is dense with vegetation, including wild ginger, guava, and giant ferns. A mosaic of sinuous tree roots lay across the muddy, and sometimes slippery, jungle path.

**Driving directions:** From Waikiki, take McCully Street to Wilder Avenue at the first traffic light after crossing over H-1. Turn left on Wilder Avenue and drive 0.4 to Punahou Street. Turn right on Punahou Street, which becomes Manoa Road, and drive 0.6 miles to a road split. Take the left fork, staying on Manoa Road to a 5-way junction at 1 mile. Curve to the right, continuing on Manoa Road past the Paradise Park parking lot. The Manoa Falls Trail is a short distance past this parking lot. Park on the short trailhead road before the main road curves sharply to the left towards Lyon Arboretum.

**Hiking directions:** Walk past the end of the road and follow the footpath slightly uphill. Cross a footbridge over Aihualama Stream. Veer left on the muddy main trail, crossing a network of tangled roots and trees draped with vines along the west bank of Waihi Stream. As you near Manoa Falls, the valley narrows and the trail steepens. Thirty yards before the falls, Aihualama Trail (Hike 8) branches sharply to the left, connecting with the Mount Tantalus trails. (A few feet up the Aihualama

Trail is a great overview of the falls and pool.) Continue on the main trail to the base of Manoa Falls at the pool. Return on the same route.

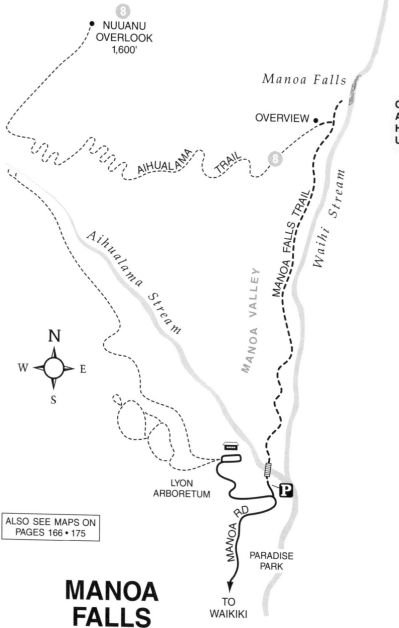

**8** NUUANU
OVERLOOK
1,600'

*Manoa Falls*

OVERVIEW •

O
A
H
U

AIHUALAMA TRAIL **8**

MANOA FALLS TRAIL

*Waihi Stream*

*Aihualama Stream*

MANOA VALLEY

N
W E
S

LYON
ARBORETUM

P

MANOA RD

PARADISE
PARK

ALSO SEE MAPS ON
PAGES 166 • 175

**MANOA
FALLS**

TO
WAIKIKI

# Hike 8
# Aihualama Trail to Nuuanu Overlook

**Hiking distance:** 5.6 miles round trip
**Hiking time:** 3 hours
**Elevation gain:** 1,100 feet
**Maps:** U.S.G.S. Honolulu
  Oahu Reference Maps: Honolulu/Oahu South Shore
  Honolulu Mauka Trail System map

**Summary of hike:** The Aihualama Trail begins at Manoa Falls (Hike 7), skirts the upper end of Manoa Valley, then heads steeply up to Pauoa Flats and a stunning overlook. The route passes through groves of bamboo, koa, eucalyptus, and enormous banyan trees. The are great views across the valley to Waikiki and Diamond Head. From the Nuuanu Overlook at the trail's end are panoramic vistas overlooking the Nuuanu Valley and the rugged Koolau Mountains.

**Driving directions:** From Waikiki, take McCully Street to Wilder Avenue at the first traffic light after crossing over H-1. Turn left on Wilder Avenue and drive 0.4 to Punahou Street. Turn right on Punahou Street, which becomes Manoa Road, and drive 0.6 miles to a road split. Take the left fork, staying on Manoa Road to a 5-way junction at 1 mile. Curve to the right, continuing on Manoa Road past the Paradise Park parking lot. The Manoa Falls Trail is a short distance past this parking lot. Park on the short trailhead road before the main road curves sharply to the left towards Lyon Arboretum.

**Hiking directions:** Follow the hiking directions to Manoa Falls—Hike 7. Just before reaching the waterfall and pool is a junction on the left with the Aihualama Trail. Bear left and head uphill a short distance to a great overview of Manoa Falls and pool. Follow the contours of the hillside, crossing several gullies to views overlooking Manoa Valley, Waahila Ridge, and Waikiki. Ascend fourteen sharp switchbacks out of Manoa Valley to a ridge in a large bamboo forest. At the ridge the

Aihualama Trail ends at a signed junction with the Puu Ohia Trail on Pauoa Flats. Take the right fork 0.7 miles through a maze of exposed tree roots, bamboo, and eucalyptus groves to the end of the trail at the Nuuanu Overlook. Return on the same trail.

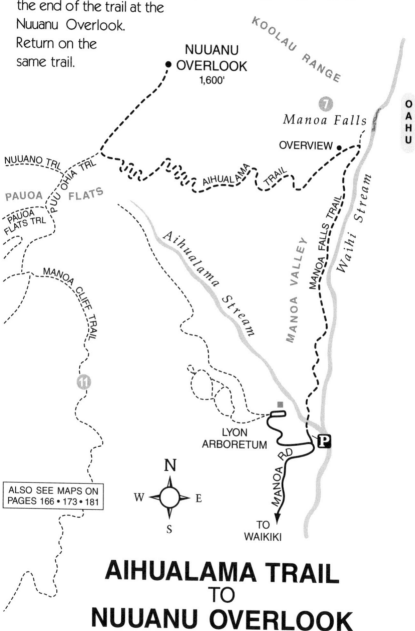

# AIHUALAMA TRAIL
## TO
# NUUANU OVERLOOK

# Hike 9
## Makiki Valley Loop

**Hiking distance:** 2 miles round trip
**Hiking time:** 1 hour
**Elevation gain:** 550 feet
**Maps:** U.S.G.S. Honolulu
Oahu Reference Maps: Honolulu/Oahu South Shore
Honolulu Mauka Trail System Maps

**Summary of hike:** The Makiki Valley Loop is located in the lush tropical forest of Makiki Valley. The paths loops on three trails through eucalyptus and bamboo groves up, across, and back down the valley. There are several stream crossings and scenic views of Honolulu and the Manoa Valley.

**Driving directions:** From Waikiki, take McCully Street to Wilder Avenue at the first traffic light after crossing over H-1. Turn left on Wilder Avenue, and drive 0.6 miles to Makiki Street. Turn right and go 0.3 miles to a road fork at the triangular-shaped Archie Baker Park. Curve to the left and continue 0.4 miles to a sharp, curving switchback to the left. Do not take the switchback. Instead, go straight (north) onto the smaller road which leads into Makiki Valley. Park on the side of the road by the park, just below the Hawaii Nature Center.

**Hiking directions:** From the end of the road, pass the Hawaii Nature Center and the forestry baseyard to the trailhead. Take the signed Kanealole Trail up the Makiki Valley. Walk through the shady forest along the west side of Kanealole Stream. The trail ends at 0.7 miles by a signed junction with the Makiki Valley Trail. Bear right, crossing several branches of Kanealole Stream. Continue across the Makiki Valley, contouring around the ridges and gullies to Moleka Stream. Cross a footbridge over the stream to a posted four-way junction with the Maunalaha and Ualakaa Trails. Take the Maunalaha Trail to the right, following the east ridge of the valley through oak, guava, and eucalyptus groves. Slowly descend to Kanealole Stream.

Wind through a forest of Norfolk Island and Cook pines, and cross a footbridge over the stream, returning to the trailhead at the nature center.

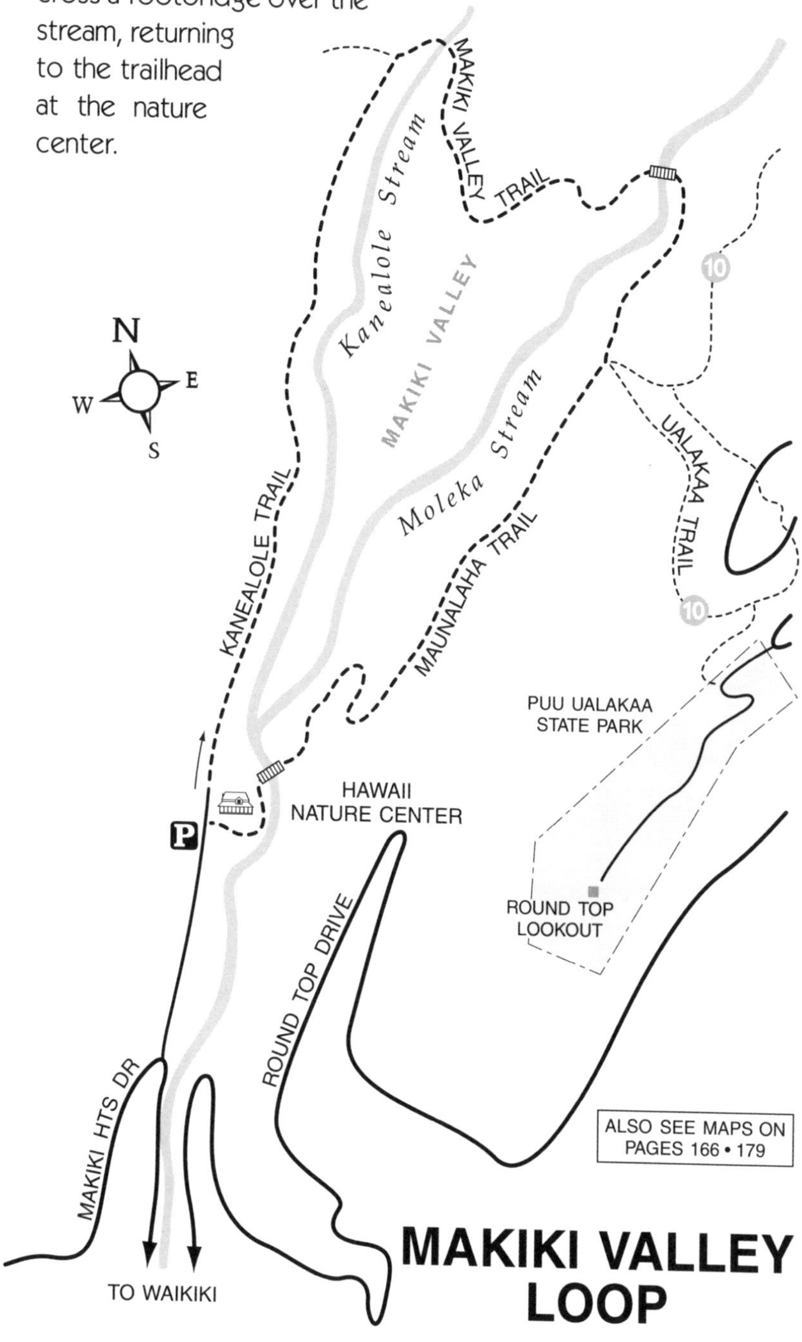

N
W E
S

MAKIKI VALLEY TRAIL

Kanealole Stream

MAKIKI VALLEY

Moleka Stream

KANEALOLE TRAIL

MAUNALAHA TRAIL

UALAKAA TRAIL

10

10

O A H U

PUU UALAKAA STATE PARK

P

HAWAII NATURE CENTER

ROUND TOP DRIVE

ROUND TOP LOOKOUT

MAKIKI HTS DR

TO WAIKIKI

ALSO SEE MAPS ON PAGES 166 • 179

# MAKIKI VALLEY LOOP

# Hike 10
# Moleka and Ualakaa Trails

**Hiking distance:** 2 miles round trip
**Hiking time:** 1 hour
**Elevation gain:** 350 feet
**Maps:** U.S.G.S. Honolulu
          Honolulu Mauka Trail System Map
          Oahu Reference Maps: Honolulu/Oahu South Shore

**Summary of hike:** The Moleka and Ualakaa Trails were established by the Sierra Club in 1979 and 1980. The two trails traverse the hillside through the upper east edge of Makiki Valley, with panoramic views down the valley. Both paths wind past large banyan trees and through forests of bamboo, ginger, ti, and lobster claw. The looping Ualakaa Trail connects the Makiki Valley Trail (Hike 9) with Puu Ualakaa State Park.

**Driving directions:** From Waikiki, take McCully Street to Wilder Avenue at the first traffic light after crossing over H-1. Turn left on Wilder Avenue and drive 0.6 miles to Makiki Street. Turn right and go 0.3 miles to a road fork at the triangular-shaped Archie Baker Park. Curve to the right onto Round Top Drive, and continue 4.3 miles up the curving road to the signed trailhead parking spaces on the left.

**Hiking directions:** Head down the well-defined Moleka Trail through the dense forest. Traverse the hillside, overlooking the Makiki Valley and the ocean below, to a T-junction at 0.7 miles. Begin the loop to the right, reaching a posted four-way junction with the Makiki Valley, Maunalaha, and Ualakaa Trails. Take the Ualakaa Trail to the left, winding through the forest. The path crosses Round Top Drive and reenters the forest directly across the road. Continue through the shade of the jungle to a second crossing of Round Top Drive. Walk up the road about 50 yards and reenter the dense forest again. Pass huge banyan trees to the T-junction, completing the loop. Return to the right on the Moleka Trail.

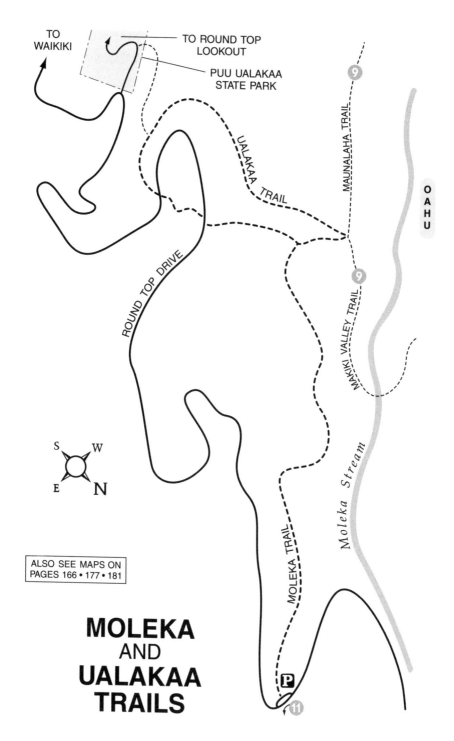

TO
WAIKIKI

TO ROUND TOP
LOOKOUT

PUU UALAKAA
STATE PARK

9

MAUNALAHA TRAIL

UALAKAA TRAIL

O A H U

ROUND TOP DRIVE

9

MAKIKI VALLEY TRAIL

S W
E N

Moleka Stream

ALSO SEE MAPS ON
PAGES 166 • 177 • 181

MOLEKA TRAIL

# MOLEKA
AND
## UALAKAA
## TRAILS

P

11

# Hike 11
## Manoa Cliff—Kalawahine Loop

**Hiking distance:** 4.8 mile loop
**Hiking time:** 2.5 hours
**Elevation gain:** 900 feet
**Maps:** U.S.G.S. Honolulu
Oahu Reference Maps: Honolulu/Oahu South Shore
Honolulu Mauka Trail System map

**Summary of hike:** The Manoa Cliff and Kalawahine Trails loop around Tantalus Crater. The hike begins on the Manoa Cliff Trail at Round Top Drive and traverses a spectacular precipice on the west side of Manoa Valley. The Kalawahine Trail returns along the northwest flank of Tantalus on the forested cliffs above Pauoa Valley, exiting at Tantalus Drive. En route, there are great views of Manoa Valley, the Koolau Range, Pearl Harbor, and Pearl City.

**Driving directions:** From Waikiki, take McCully Street to Wilder Avenue at the first traffic light after crossing over H-1. Turn left on Wilder Avenue, and drive 0.6 miles to Makiki Street. Turn right and go 0.3 miles to a road fork at the triangular-shaped Archie Baker Park. Curve to the right onto Round Top Drive, and continue 4.3 miles up the curving road to the signed Moleka Trail parking spaces on the left.

**Hiking directions:** The signed Manoa Cliff Trail begins across the road to the north. Enter the lush forest, gaining gradual but steady elevation. The well-defined path climbs some steps and winds up the mountain. Follow the edge of the cliff past a number of vista points overlooking Manoa Valley to the east. Descend to a signed junction with the Puu Ohia Trail at 1.4 miles. Stay on the Manoa Cliff Trail straight ahead on the right fork, gradually descending 0.2 miles to a junction and trail map with the Pauoa Flats Trail on the right. Stay left through the ginger and fern-lined path, heading down switchbacks to a junction with the Kalawahine Trail a half mile ahead. Bear left, curving along the contours of the mountainside above Pauoa Valley for 1.1 miles. Reach the trail's end at Tantalus Drive. Follow the road 1.5 miles to the left (east) back to the trailhead.

Note: The park maps refer to the entire trail as Manoa Cliff but the signage along the route designates the last portion as the Kalawahine Trail.

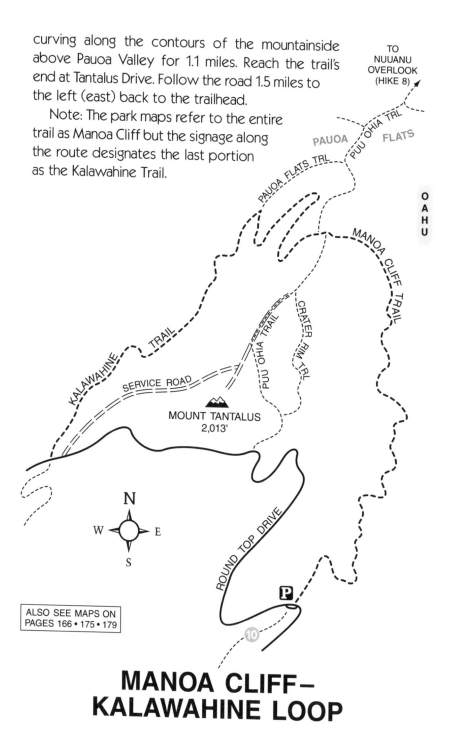

TO NUUANU OVERLOOK (HIKE 8)

PAUOA FLATS

PUU OHIA TRL

PAUOA FLATS TRL

MANOA CLIFF TRAIL

O A H U

KALAWAHINE TRAIL

PUU OHIA TRAIL

CRATER RIM TRL

SERVICE ROAD

MOUNT TANTALUS
2,013'

N
W      E
S

ROUND TOP DRIVE

P

10

ALSO SEE MAPS ON
PAGES 166 • 175 • 179

# MANOA CLIFF–
# KALAWAHINE LOOP

# Hike 12
## Judd Memorial Trail
## to Jackass Ginger Pool

**Hiking distance:** 1 mile loop
**Hiking time:** 1 hour
**Elevation gain:** 200 feet
**Maps:** U.S.G.S. Honolulu
Oahu Reference Maps: Honolulu/Oahu South Shore
Honolulu Mauka Trail System map

**Summary of hike:** The Judd Memorial Trail is a short loop hike in the Nuuanu Valley. The path crosses the Nuuanu Stream and traverses the north-facing hillside through bamboo, eucalyptus, and Norfolk Island pine groves. A side path leads down to Jackass Ginger Pool, a large circular pool with a 10-foot waterfall cascading over rocks into the pool.

**Driving directions:** From Waikiki, take H-1 west 1.5 miles to the Pali Highway (61) north. Drive 2.5 miles on the Pali Highway to the Nuuanu Pali Drive exit. Take the turnoff to the right, and stay on Nuuanu Pali Drive for one mile to the signed trailhead parking lot on the right. If the lot is closed, park along the side of the road.

**Hiking directions:** Descend towards Nuuanu Stream. Rock-hop across the stream to a junction at the signed Judd Trail. Begin the loop on the left fork through a giant bamboo grove. The serpentine path gains elevation, traversing the hillside above the stream through eucalyptus and Norfolk Island pines. Descend and cross a small gully to a signed trail with the Nuuanu Trail on the left. Stay to the right on the Judd Trail, and drop back down the hill. As you reach a residential area, the path curves right and begins returning high above and parallel to Nuuanu Stream. Watch for a metal stake marking a side path on the left. Take this short, steep side path 25 yards to Jackass Ginger Pool. After enjoying the pool, return to the Judd Trail and bear left. Additional side paths on the left lead down to smaller pools with cascades and waterfalls. The main trail slopes gradually down to Nuuanu Stream, completing the loop. Before recrossing the stream to the trailhead, follow the watercourse about 10 yards upstream to another waterfall.

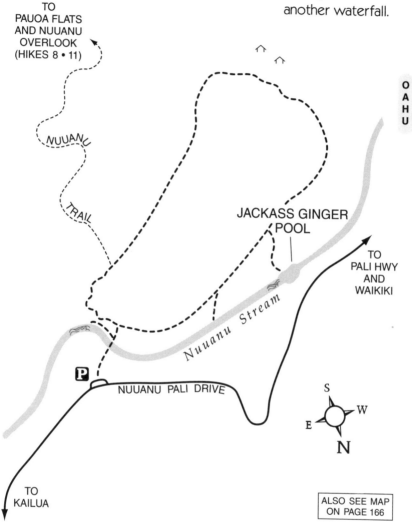

# JUDD MEMORIAL TRAIL
## TO
# JACKASS GINGER POOL

# Hike 13
# Old Pali Road and Pali Lookout

**Hiking distance:** 2 miles round trip
**Hiking time:** 1 hour
**Elevation gain:** 350 feet
**Maps:** U.S.G.S. Honolulu
        Oahu Reference Maps: Central Oahu/Windward Coast

**Summary of hike:** This hike heads downhill along an abandoned portion of the Old Pali Highway built in 1932. The area is lush with vegetation that is slowly taking over the road. The trail begins at the Pali Lookout on the summit of the Koolau Mountains. From the clifftop perch are sweeping vistas of Windward Oahu from an elevation of 1,200 feet. It overlooks the towns and bays of Kailua and Kaneohe. These spectacular, unobstructed views extend across the vertical ridges, tall forbidding peaks, and deep valleys of the sheer Pali cliffs to the coastal plain and ocean below. The lookout is often windy but the views are staggering.

**Driving directions:** From Waikiki, take H-1 west 1.5 miles to the Pali Highway (61) north. Drive 5.4 miles north to the signed Pali Lookout and Nuuanu Pali State Park exit on the right. Exit and continue 0.3 miles to the state park parking lot.

**Hiking directions:** Walk to the brink of the cliffs on the Pali Lookout platform. On each side of the lookout are paths that meet at the lower lookout level. Go to the right past a gate, and begin a gentle descent with lush cliffs on the right and the commanding views toward the sea and Kaneohe Bay on the left. As you near the Pali Highway, the wide old road narrows to a footpath that weaves between fallen boulders from the eroded cliffs above. This is the turnaround spot. Return along the same path.

    To hike further, the trail continues, connecting with the Maunawili Demonstration Trail (Hike 14) 0.7 miles further.

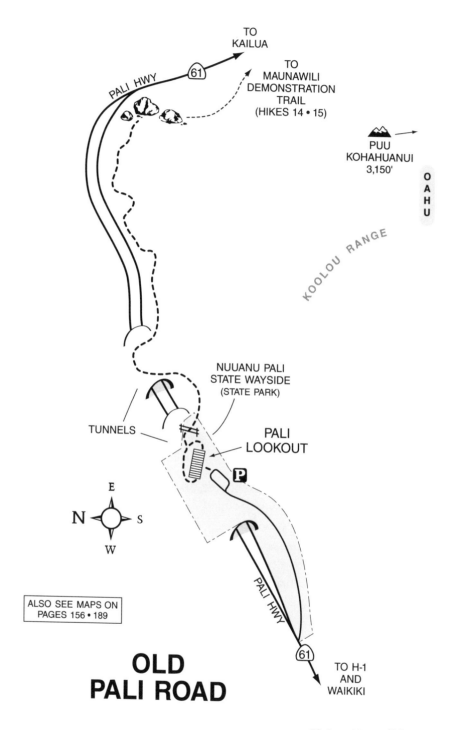

TO
KAILUA

PALI HWY (61)

TO
MAUNAWILI
DEMONSTRATION
TRAIL
(HIKES 14 • 15)

PUU
KOHAHUANUI
3,150'

O A H U

KOOLOU RANGE

NUUANU PALI
STATE WAYSIDE
(STATE PARK)

TUNNELS

PALI
LOOKOUT

P

E

N  S

W

ALSO SEE MAPS ON
PAGES 156 • 189

PALI HWY

(61)

TO H-1
AND
WAIKIKI

# OLD
# PALI ROAD

# Hike 14
## Maunawili Demonstration Trail
### WEST TRAILHEAD FROM NUUANU PALI LOOKOUT

**Hiking distance:** 4 miles round trip
**Hiking time:** 2 hours
**Elevation gain:** 300 feet
**Maps:** U.S.G.S. Honolulu and Koko Head
　　　　Oahu Reference Maps: Central Oahu/Windward Coast

map
next page

**Summary of hike:** The Maunawili Demonstration Trail is a well-defined tropical forest hike with scenic vistas across the windward side of the Koolau Range. The 9.3-mile trail connects the Nuuanu Pali Lookout with Waimanalo on the windward coast, circling around the three distinct peaks of Mount Olomana to the northeast. This hike follows the first two miles of the trail along the north wall of Maunawili Valley on the lush slopes of the Koolau Mountains. The hike can be combined with the trail from the Waimanalo trailhead (Hike 15) for a 9.3-mile, one-way shuttle hike.

**Driving directions:** From Waikiki, take H-1 west 1.5 miles to the Pali Highway (61) north. Drive 6.9 miles north, passing through two tunnels, to the signed "Scenic Point" turnout on the right. Park in the turnout.

**Hiking directions:** Walk back to the top of the turnout by the opening in the guard rail. Take the footpath past the trail sign into the lush tropical forest with an understory of ferns and jungle vines. Pass green, moss-covered rocks, following the contours of the mountain past a junction on the right to Nuuanu Pali State Wayside (Hike 13). Cross gullies and drainages with footbridges, boardwalks, and numerous trickling streams. Pass a water tank on the right by an overlook of Kailua and the ocean. Zigzag down into the wet, lush gullies, then cross over ridges with vistas of the surrounding mountains. This up and down route of lush drainages and ridges with differing scenic views continues for miles. Choose your own turnaround spot.

# Hike 15
## Maunawili Demonstration Trail
### EAST TRAILHEAD FROM WAIMANALO

**Hiking distance:** 2.6 miles round trip
**Hiking time:** 1.5 hours
**Elevation gain:** 450 feet
**Maps:** U.S.G.S. Koko Head
      Oahu Reference Maps: Central Oahu/Windward Coast

map
next page

O
A
H
U

**Summary of hike:** The Maunawili Demonstration Trail is a 9.3-mile trail from Waimanalo to Nuuanu Pali Lookout on the Pali Highway. This hike follows the first 1.3 miles of the trail from the east trailhead to the Aniani Nui Ridge, the south ridge descending from Mount Olomana. The hike can be combined with the trail from the Nuuanu Pali Lookout Trailhead (Hike 14) for a one-way shuttle hike. (For the shuttle hike, it is easier to begin from the Pali Highway—Hike 14—and walk downhill.)

**Driving directions:** From Waikiki, take H–1 west 1.5 miles to the Pali Highway (61) north. Drive 9.5 miles north to the end of the Pali Highway in Kailua, where the Pali Highway crosses the Kalanianaole Highway (72) and becomes Kailua Road. Turn right on Highway 72, and drive 3.1 miles to Kumuhau Street on the right, just past the Olomana Golf Course. Turn right on Kumuhau Street, and go 1 mile to a T-junction with Waikupanaha Street. Turn right and continue 0.2 miles to the signed trailhead on the right by the gated fenceline. Park in the pullout.

**Hiking directions:** Walk past the signed trail gate and take the wide jeep road uphill through the lush forest to a posted junction at 0.2 miles. The right fork follows the Maunawili Ditch Trail (an easy sidetrip). Stay on the Maunawili Demonstration Trail, continuing straight ahead on the main path. At a half mile the trail bends sharply to the right to a trail split and a "no horse access" sign. The right fork passes metal posts to a footpath. Stay to the left as the footpath narrows and follows the edge of the cliffs, overlooking the Koolau Mountains, the Waimanalo

Valley, and Manana Island. Wind along the edge of the mountain into the shady forest. The path crosses the Aniani Nui Ridge and emerges at a steep road and four-way junction at 1.3 miles. This is a good turnaround spot.

To hike further, cross the road and continue on the signed Maunawili Demonstration Trail.

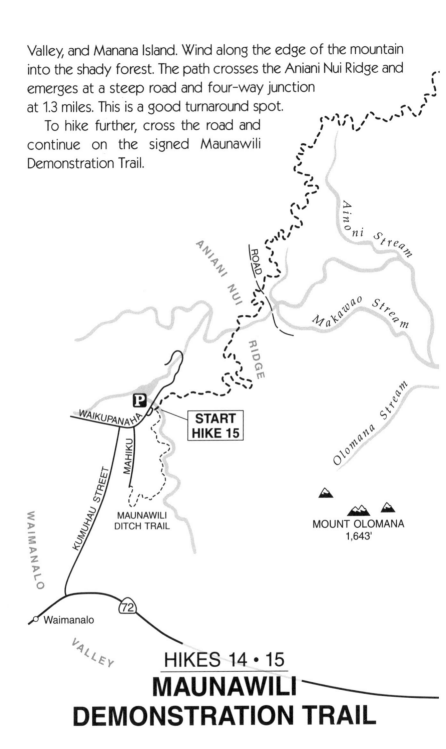

HIKES 14 • 15
# MAUNAWILI
# DEMONSTRATION TRAIL

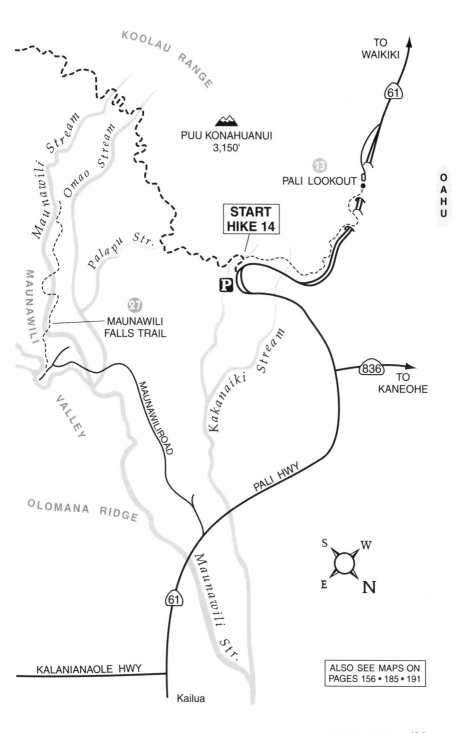

KOOLAU RANGE

Maunawili Stream

Omao Stream

PUU KONAHUANUI
3,150'

TO WAIKIKI

61

13
PALI LOOKOUT

OAHU

Palapu Str.

START
HIKE 14

P

MAUNAWILI

27
MAUNAWILI
FALLS TRAIL

Kakanaiki Stream

836
TO KANEOHE

VALLEY

MAUNAWILIROAD

PALI HWY

OLOMANA RIDGE

S    W

E    N

61

Maunawili Str.

KALANIANAOLE HWY

Kailua

ALSO SEE MAPS ON
PAGES 156 • 185 • 191

# Hike 16
# Maunawili Falls

**Hiking distance:** 2.6 miles round trip
**Hiking time:** 1:45 hours
**Elevation gain:** 400 feet
**Maps:** U.S.G.S. Koko Head and Honolulu
　　　　Oahu Reference Maps: Central Oahu/Windward Coast

**Summary of hike:** Maunawili Falls is an alluring 20-foot cataract that cascades off rocky cliffs into a deep pool. The trail to Maunawili Falls is set in a beautiful forest on the slopes of the Koolau Mountains near the town of Maunawili. The path follows Maunawili Stream; the cascading sounds of the stream are constant throughout the hike. The forested area is rich with banana, papaya, ginger, ti, and taro plants.

**Driving directions:** From Waikiki, take H-1 west to the Pali Highway (61) north. Drive 9 miles to the second Auloa Road turnoff—turn right. At 0.1 mile the road forks. Take the left fork—Maunawili Road. Continue 1.5 miles to the trailhead on the left. Park alongside the curb on Kelewina Street on the right.

**Hiking directions:** The posted trailhead begins by following an asphalt road about 100 yards to a footpath on the right. Take this footpath, which parallels and crosses Maunawili Stream using rocks as stepping stones. At 0.7 miles, a little over half way, is the third crossing of the stream. From here it is a short climb to a signed junction on a ridge with views of the surrounding Koolau Mountains. Take the left fork and descend to the stream. Boulder hop upstream a short distance to the falls and swimming pool. Return along the same trail.

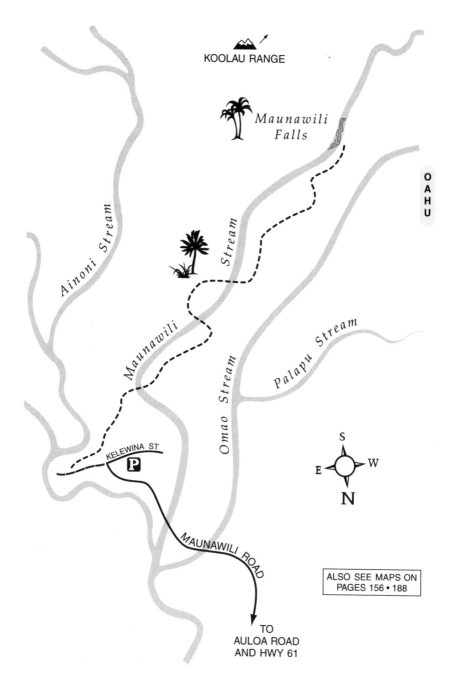

KOOLAU RANGE

OAHU

Maunawili
Falls

Ainoni Stream

Stream

Maunawili

Palapu Stream

Omao Stream

KELEWINA ST

P

S

E W

N

MAUNAWILI ROAD

TO
AULOA ROAD
AND HWY 61

ALSO SEE MAPS ON
PAGES 156 • 188

# MAUNAWILI FALLS

# Hike 17
# Hoomaluhia Botanical Garden

45-680 Luluku Road, Kaneohe
Open daily · 9 a.m.—4 p.m.

**Hiking distance:** 1—2 miles
**Hiking time:** 1 hour (plus browsing time)
**Elevation gain:** Near level
**Maps:** U.S.G.S. Kaneeohe
Botanical Garden Map (available at visitor center)

**Summary of hike:** Hoomaluhia Botanical Garden is situated on 400 sloping acres of former farmland in windward Oahu above Kaneohe. The rainforest garden sits at the foot of the Koolau Mountains beneath the towering Pali Cliffs. An ocean view spreads out to the northeast. The verdant garden serves as a nature conservancy, yet looks more like a natural forest reserve. There are hundreds of flowers, fruits, bushes, vines, and trees from tropical regions all over the world. The gardens include a 32-acre manmade lake, streams, footbridges, meadows, a visitor center, picnic pavilions, and a network of meandering trails along the lush Koolau foothills.

**Driving directions:** From Waikiki, take H-1 west 1.5 miles to the Pali Highway (61) north. Drive 7.7 miles north to the junction with the Kamehameha Highway (83) and turn left. Continue 2 miles and turn left on Luluku Road. Drive 1.6 miles to the parking lot and visitor center inside the botanical garden.

**Hiking directions:** From the visitor center, take the walking path past a few small buildings. The trail continues along the south side of Loko Waimaluhia, a 32-acre reservoir and dam. Paths follow along streams, over footbridges, and in and around the gardens. Explore on your own, choosing your own route and turnaround spot.

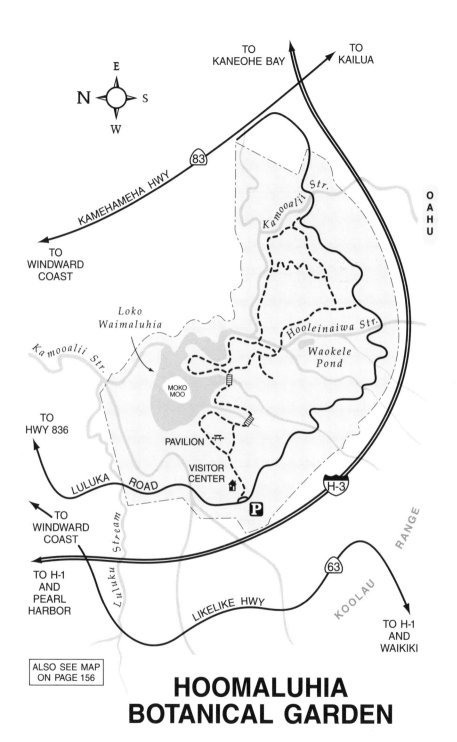

TO
KANEOHE BAY

TO
KAILUA

E
N S
W

83
KAMEHAMEHA HWY

TO
WINDWARD
COAST

*Kamooalii Str.*

*Str.*

OAHU

*Loko Waimaluhia*

*Kamooalii Str.*

*Hooleinaiwa Str.*

*Waokele Pond*

MOKO
MOO

TO
HWY 836

PAVILION

VISITOR
CENTER

LULUKA ROAD

P

H-3

TO
WINDWARD
COAST

TO H-1
AND
PEARL
HARBOR

*Luluku Stream*

RANGE

63

LIKELIKE HWY

KOOLAU

TO H-1
AND
WAIKIKI

ALSO SEE MAP
ON PAGE 156

# HOOMALUHIA
# BOTANICAL GARDEN

# Hike 18
# Aiea Loop Trail
## KEAIWA HEIAU STATE PARK

**Hiking distance:** 5 miles round trip
**Hiking time:** 3 hours
**Elevation gain:** 1,000 feet
**Maps:** U.S.G.S. Waipahu and Kaneohe

**Summary of hike:** Keaiwa Heiau State Park is the site of an ancient healing temple. The park sits in the foothills of the Koolau Range above the town of Aiea. The Aiea Loop Trail snakes along a ridge descending from the Koolau Mountains in the state park. The trail winds through tall forests of eucalyptus, Norfolk Island, koa, ohia, ironwood, and guava trees. The well-maintained path passes numerous majestic canyons and has great views of Pearl Harbor, the Koolau Range, and Central Oahu.

**Driving directions:** From Waikiki, take H-1 west to Highway 78 and Aiea. (Stay in the left lanes for the Highway 78 junction.) From Highway 78, take the Aiea exit onto Moanalua Road. From Moanalua Road, turn right on Aiea Heights Drive. Aiea Heights Drive winds its way into Keaiwa Heiau State Park. Drive on this one-way road to its highest point, and park in the parking lot by the trailhead.

**Hiking directions:** Pick up the trail at the back of the parking lot by the water tank. Hike through the eucalyptus grove with a magnificent root system woven across the red dirt path. Shortly beyond the grove is a level, exposed viewing area of Honolulu. The trail follows the ridge with alternating views of the city on the right and the seemingly endless Koolau Range on the left. Disregard the numerous side paths that descend from the ridge. Continue east to Puu Uau, the highest and easternmost point of the trail. As you pass the far end of the loop, watch the gully for wreckage of a C47 cargo plane from a 1943 crash. Gradually descend to the Aiea Stream. As you near the end of the hike, switchbacks lead out of the gulch to the ridge. Enter a camping area, and climb steps to a parking lot and spur road. Follow the spur road to the main park road, and bear to the right, returning to the trailhead.

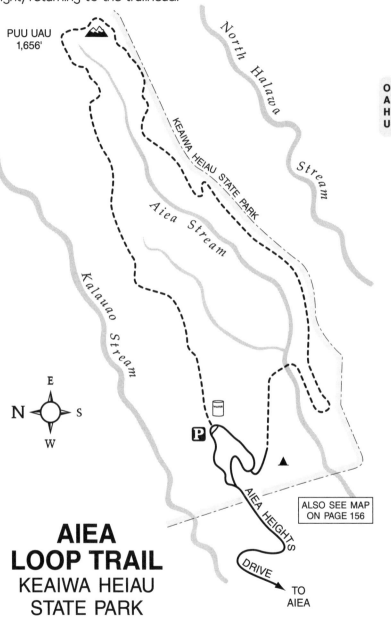

PUU UAU
1,656'

North Halawa Stream

O A H U

KEAIWA HEIAU STATE PARK

Aiea Stream

Kalauao Stream

E
N — S
W

WATER

P

ALSO SEE MAP
ON PAGE 156

AIEA HEIGHTS
DRIVE
TO
AIEA

**AIEA
LOOP TRAIL**
KEAIWA HEIAU
STATE PARK

# Hike 19
# Upper and Lower Waimano Loop Trail

**Hiking distance:** 2 mile loop
**Hiking time:** 1 hour
**Elevation gain:** 300 feet
**Maps:** U.S.G.S. Waipahu
   Oahu Reference Maps: Central Oahu/Windward Coast

**Summary of hike:** This pleasant trail makes a loop through the forested Waimano Valley. The upper trail traverses the hillside above the valley, following an abandoned irrigation ditch through groves of guava and mahogany trees with an understory of ferns. The return route on the lower trail parallels Waimano Stream along the valley floor.

**Driving directions:** From Waikiki, take H-1 west 11 miles to Exit 10/Pearl City. The exit curves to the right onto Moanalua Road, heading northwest. Drive one mile to the road's end. Turn right and continue 1.7 miles on Waimano Home Road to the signed trailhead parking area on the left. The trailhead is located by the security gate at Waimano Home.

**Hiking directions:** Take the well-marked trail on the left side of the road and chain-link fence. Follow the fenceline 50 yards to the first junction with the Lower Waimano Trail on the left. Begin the loop to the right, staying on the upper trail. At 0.4 miles, leave the fenceline and enter the beautiful, dense forest. Climb a short, steep hill to an overlook of Waimano Canyon, Pearl City, the ocean, and at the west end of the island, the Waianae Range. Descend the north-facing cliffs parallel to an irrigation ditch on the right. Traverse the canyon wall to a signed Y-junction at one mile. The Upper Waimano Trail (Hike 20) continues to the right. Bear left on the Lower Waimano Trail, making a zigzag descent to the streambed. Return downstream through hau groves along the level canyon floor, paralleling Waimano Stream. Gradually angle up the hillside back to the ridge, completing the loop. Return to the trailhead on the right.

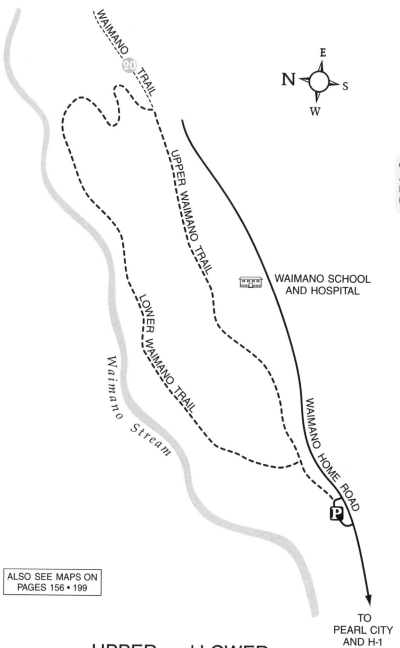

N E S W

WAIMANO TRAIL

UPPER WAIMANO TRAIL

LOWER WAIMANO TRAIL

Waimano Stream

WAIMANO SCHOOL
AND HOSPITAL

WAIMANO HOME ROAD

P

O A H U

ALSO SEE MAPS ON
PAGES 156 • 199

TO
PEARL CITY
AND H-1

# UPPER and LOWER
# WAIMANO LOOP TRAIL

# Hike 20
# Waimano Trail

**Hiking distance:** 4.5 miles round trip
**Hiking time:** 2.5 hours
**Elevation gain:** 300 feet
**Maps:** U.S.G.S. Waipahu
          Oahu Reference Maps: Central Oahu/Windward Coast

**Summary of hike:** The Waimano Trail is a forested seven-mile trail that climbs 1,600 feet to a perch high atop the Koolau Mountains. This shorter hike takes in the first couple of miles, heading deeply into the mountains above Waimano Valley. The cliffside trail leads to an overlook of the valley on a ridge with a picnic shelter in a eucalyptus grove.

**Driving directions:** Follow the driving directions for Hike 19.

**Hiking directions:** Take the signed path on the left side of the road, following the fenceline to the first junction with the Lower Waimano Trail (Hike 19). Stay on the upper trail along the fenceline. The path leaves the fenceline and enters the lush shady forest at 0.4 miles. Climb a short, steep hill to an overlook of Waimano Canyon, Pearl City, the ocean, and the Waianae Range. Descend the north-facing cliffs parallel to a water ditch on the right. Traverse the canyon wall to the second junction with the Lower Waimano Trail on the left at one mile. Stay to the right, crossing small sections of the rock-wall ditch through the deep jungle. The trail narrows on a steep cliff. Careful footing is required, with little room for error. At two miles cross a seasonal stream at the ruins of an old diversion dam. Curve to the right and ascend the hillside on the north canyon wall, curving left towards the ridge. Just below the ridge, a switchback on the left leads to a Boy Scout picnic shelter and overlook. This is our turnaround spot.

To hike further, the main trail follows the ridge, descending to another dam and pool at 3 miles, then steadily climbs to the crest of the Koolau Range at 7 miles.

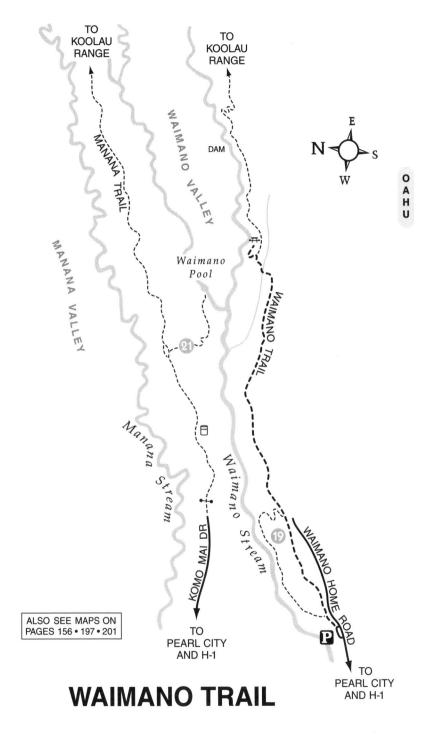

TO
KOOLAU
RANGE

TO
KOOLAU
RANGE

WAIMANO VALLEY

DAM

MANANA TRAIL

MANANA VALLEY

*Waimano Pool*

E
N ☼ S
W

O A H U

WAIMANO TRAIL

21

*Manana Stream*

*Waimano Stream*

19

WAIMANO HOME ROAD

KOMO MAI DR

ALSO SEE MAPS ON
PAGES 156 • 197 • 201

TO
PEARL CITY
AND H-1

🅿

TO
PEARL CITY
AND H-1

# WAIMANO TRAIL

# Hike 21
# Manana Trail to Waimano Pool

**Hiking distance:** 3 miles round trip
**Hiking time:** 1.5 hours
**Elevation gain:** 600 feet
**Maps:** U.S.G.S. Waipahu
       Oahu Reference Maps: Central Oahu/Windward Coast

**Summary of hike:** Waimano Pool is a swimming hole with a small waterfall deep in the forest in the lush Waimano Valley. The hike follows the first mile of the Manana Trail atop the ridge that overlooks Manana Valley and Waimano Valley. A steep side path descends into the Waimano Valley to the stream and pool on the valley floor.

**Driving directions:** From Waikiki, take H-1 west 11 miles to Exit 10/Pearl City. The exit curves to the right onto Moanalua Road, heading northwest. Drive one mile to the road's end. Turn right and continue 0.6 miles on Waimano Home Road to the second stop light at Komo Mai Drive. Turn left and go 3.1 miles to the end of the road.

**Hiking directions:** Take the signed trailhead at the end of the road. Pass the trail gate on the paved path into the forest. The paved road ends at a water tank on the right at 0.4 miles. Continue northeast along the ridge on the footpath, crossing under two sets of power lines. Various hunter trails veer off the ridge into Manana Valley on the left and Waimano Valley on the right. Stay on the ridge, overlooking both stream-fed jungle canyons. Descend to the base of a large knoll and an unsigned trail fork at one mile. The Manana Trail curves around the right side of the knoll, returning to the ridge. The path to the pool stays to the right on a distinct trail along the side ridge. Begin the steep descent into Waimano Valley. This steep trail is known locally as "Heart Attack Hill." A rope tied to trailside trees is available for better grip on the steep sections. As you descend, curve left, staying on the main trail. Avoid the temptation of bearing to the right, directly toward the stream. At Waimano Stream, take the left fork a short distance upstream to Waimano Pool and a small waterfall.

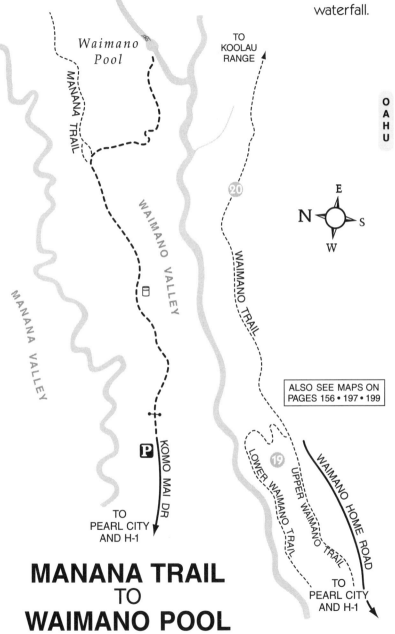

*Waimano Pool*

TO KOOLAU RANGE

MANANA TRAIL

WAIMANO VALLEY

MANANA VALLEY

WAIMANO TRAIL

20

19

LOWER WAIMANO TRAIL

UPPER WAIMANO TRAIL

WAIMANO HOME ROAD

**O A H U**

E
N — S
W

ALSO SEE MAPS ON
PAGES 156 • 197 • 199

P

KOMO MAI DR

TO
PEARL CITY
AND H-1

TO
PEARL CITY
AND H-1

# MANANA TRAIL
## TO
# WAIMANO POOL

# Hike 22
# Wahiawa Botanic Garden
### 1396 California Avenue, Wahiawa
### Open daily · 9 a.m. — 4 p.m.

**Hiking distance:** 1 mile round trip
**Hiking time:** 1 hour
**Elevation gain:** 50 feet
**Maps:** U.S.G.S. Hauula
Oahu Reference Maps: Central Oahu/Windward Coast
Wahiawa Botanical Garden map

**Summary of hike:** Wahiawa Botanic Garden in central Oahu is one of the five Honolulu Botanical Gardens. The 27-acre garden dates back to the 1920s when the Hawaii Sugar Planters Association leased the land for experimental tree planting. The garden is tucked into a lush, forested ravine at an elevation of 1,000 feet. The cool yet humid garden includes a tropical rain-forest, native trees, and exotic trees from Africa, Asia, Australia, China, Japan, New Guinea, and the Philippines.

**Driving directions:** From Waikiki, take H-1 west for 16 miles to Exit 8, the H-2/Wahiawa exit. Drive 8 miles north on H-2 to Highway 80 (Kamehameha Highway) in Wahiawa. Bear right on Highway 80 and go 0.4 miles to the third traffic light at California Avenue. Turn right and continue 0.9 miles to the botanical garden and parking lot on the left.

**Hiking directions:** Before entering the botanic garden, walk to the west end of the parking lot. A bridge spans the gulch, overlooking the magnificent gardens. Return to the entrance building at the east end of the parking lot, and take the paved path winding down the slope into the densely wooded ravine. At the canyon floor, a labyrinth of footpaths weave through the gardens with flowering trees entangled by vines and rich green ferns. Some of the paths are lined with bamboo railings. With so much to explore, meander at your own pace and choose your own route.

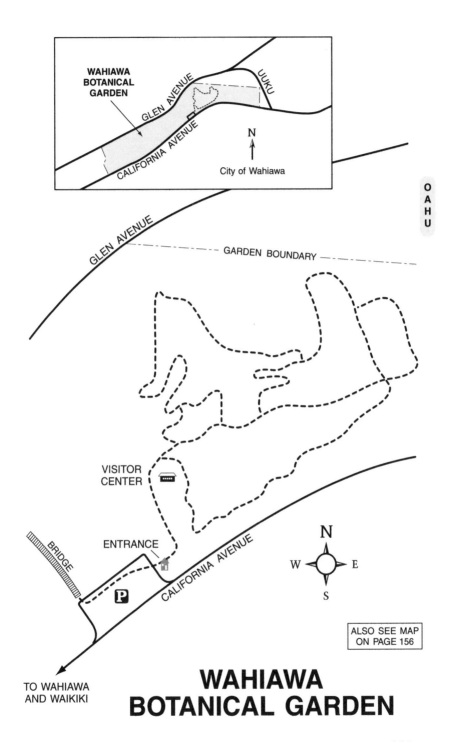

GLEN AVENUE

UUKU

N

City of Wahiawa

OAHU

GLEN AVENUE

GARDEN BOUNDARY

VISITOR
CENTER

BRIDGE

ENTRANCE

CALIFORNIA AVENUE

P

N

W

E

S

ALSO SEE MAP
ON PAGE 156

TO WAHIAWA
AND WAIKIKI

# WAHIAWA
# BOTANICAL GARDEN

# Hike 23
## Kaena Point—south access

**Hiking distance:** 5 miles round trip
**Hiking time:** 2.5 hours
**Elevation gain:** Level
**Maps:** U.S.G.S. Kaena
        Oahu Reference Maps: North Shore/Leeward Coast

map
next page

**Summary of hike:** Kaena Point is a narrow peninsula at the westernmost tip of Oahu. The Waianae Range tapers to the point, ending at the remote twelve-acre Kaena Point Natural Area Reserve. The exposed reserve is covered with wind-swept dunes, a string of shoreline rocks, sparse vegetation, and a beacon. The trail, an old rutted railroad route, parallels the level volcanic coastline, passing tidepools, sea caves, natural arches, and blowholes. Kaena Point can be approached from both the south shore and north shore (Hike 24). The two paths merge at the isolated point. This hike begins at the arid south (leeward) shore at the end of the road.

**Driving directions:** From Waikiki, take H-1 west for 25 miles, curving around Pearl Harbor to the leeward coast at Kahe Point. H-1 becomes the Farrington Highway (93) a few miles before reaching the coastline. From Kahe Point, continue 19 miles parallel to the coastline to the end of the paved road at Yokohama Bay Beach. Park in large pullout on the inland side of road.

**Hiking directions:** Follow the jeep road northwest, sandwiched between the ocean cliffs and Kuaokala Ridge. The road follows the marine shelf along the scalloped coral and black lava coastline. Fingers of lava stretch out to sea with endless tidepools, overhanging rocks, natural arches, and blowholes. Railroad tie remnants from the turn of the century are visible along the path. Cross a small gulch where the road was washed out. Nearing the point, at the west end of the mountain range, is a signed junction. The right fork continues on the old road, curving around the base of the mountains to the north side of

Oahu (Hike 24). Take the left fork into the Kaena Point Natural Area on the exposed rock-lined footpath. Cross the dunes towards the beacon, which can be seen near the point. Beyond the beacon, explore the sandy point, choosing your own route.

# Hike 24
## Kaena Point—north access

**Hiking distance:** 5.5 miles round trip
**Hiking time:** 2.5 hours
**Elevation gain:** Level
**Maps:** U.S.G.S. Kaena
Oahu Reference Maps: North Shore/Leeward Coast

map
next page

O
A
H
U

**Summary of hike:** Kaena Point is located at the arid west end of Oahu. The Waianae Range tapers to a point where the north and south shores merge, forming the remote peninsula. At the point, the twelve-acre Kaena Point Natural Area Reserve protrudes across the windswept dunes past a beacon. Huge waves from both shores crash against the lava rocks that band the point. Kaena Point can be approached from either the north or south shore (Hike 23). The two paths merge at the isolated point. This hike begins on the north shore.

**Driving directions:** From Waikiki, take H-1 west for 16 miles to Exit 8, the H-2/Wahiawa exit. Drive 8 miles north on H-2 to Highway 99 in Wahiawa. Take Highway 99 for 1.5 miles to a road split with Highway 803. Bear left on Highway 803 (Kaukonahua Road) towards Waialua, and go 7 miles to Highway 930, the Farrington Highway. Bear left on Highway 930 and drive 7.5 miles to the end of the paved road. Park in the sandy pullouts on the side of the road.

**Hiking directions:** Head west on the unpaved road to the trailhead gate past large boulders. Two parallel trails lead to the point—the old rutted road and the serpentine shoreline trail. Both trails parallel the coastline past sea-cut cliffs, deserted beaches, and secluded coves. Continue west across the wide open space along the base of Kuaokala Ridge. At 2 miles, large lava boulders block the road at the gate entrance to Keana Point Natural Reserve. Pass through the gate, and continue towards the point to a trail split at the end of the mountain range. The road curves left along the talus slope, following the base of the mountain to the leeward coast. The right fork crosses the dunes towards the beacon, which can be seen near the point. Beyond the beacon, explore the awesome point, choosing your own route.

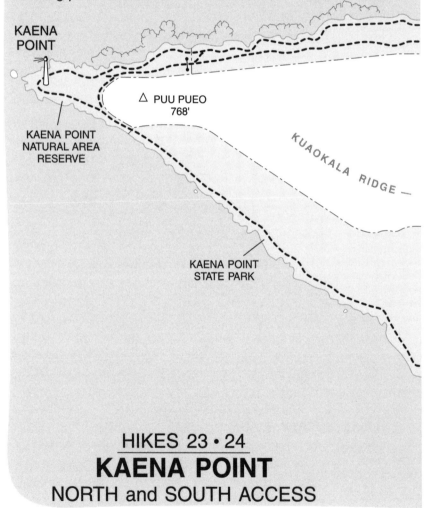

KAENA POINT

KAENA POINT
NATURAL AREA
RESERVE

△ PUU PUEO
768'

KUAOKALA RIDGE

KAENA POINT
STATE PARK

HIKES 23 • 24
# KAENA POINT
## NORTH and SOUTH ACCESS

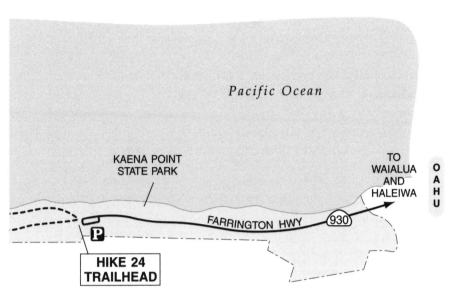

Pacific Ocean

KAENA POINT
STATE PARK

TO
WAIALUA
AND
HALEIWA

O A H U

FARRINGTON HWY (930)

P

**HIKE 24
TRAILHEAD**

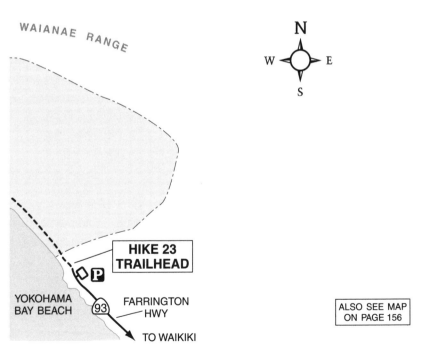

WAIANAE RANGE

N
W ←○→ E
S

**HIKE 23
TRAILHEAD**

P

YOKOHAMA
BAY BEACH (93)

FARRINGTON
HWY

TO WAIKIKI

ALSO SEE MAP
ON PAGE 156

# Hike 25
# Pupukea Beach Park

**Hiking distance:** 1.2 miles round trip
**Hiking time:** 1 hour
**Elevation gain:** Level
**Maps:** U.S.G.S. Waimea
       Oahu Reference Maps: North Shore/Leeward Coast

**Summary of hike:** Pupukea Beach Park, a Marine Life Conservation Area, is a long, narrow park adjacent to Waimea Bay. At the south end of the eighty-acre park is Three Tables, a protected beach with three sections of flat coral reefs. At the north end of the park is a wall of coral reef that forms an enclosed lagoon known as Shark's Cove. The large cove is a snorkeling and beachcombing paradise with tidepools, lava cave formations, and blowholes. A walking and biking path lines the back of the beach along an elevated grassy area with groves of ironwoods.

**Driving directions:** From Waikiki, take H-1 west for 16 miles to Exit 8, the H-2/Wahiawa exit. Drive 8 miles north on H-2 to Highway 99 in Wahiawa. Take Highway 99/Kamehameha Highway north to the Weed Circle round-about, just south of Haleiwa. Take Highway 83, the Kamehameha Highway, a short distance into the town of Haleiwa. From Haleiwa, continue 5 miles northeast on Highway 83 to the signed parking area on the ocean side of the highway, across from Foodland Market at Pupukea Road.

**Hiking directions:** Head south (left) on the walking path towards Waimea Bay. The path overlooks Three Tables and extends out to the lava rock point adjacent to Waimea Bay. Returning to the north, follow the grassy path along the back end of the beach towards Shark's Cove. At the cove, cross the coral to the enclosed pool. Explore the magnificent area, choosing your own route.

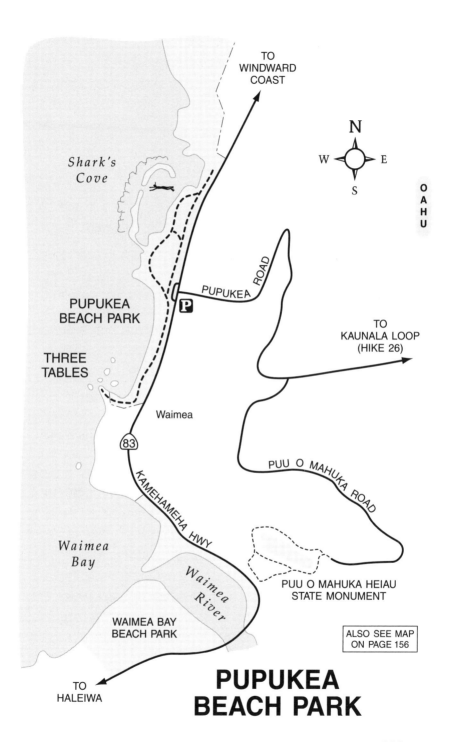

TO
WINDWARD
COAST

N
W E
S

O A H U

Shark's
Cove

PUPUKEA ROAD

P

PUPUKEA
BEACH PARK

THREE
TABLES

TO
KAUNALA LOOP
(HIKE 26)

Waimea

83

PUU O MAHUKA ROAD

KAMEHAMEHA HWY

Waimea
Bay

Waimea
River

PUU O MAHUKA HEIAU
STATE MONUMENT

ALSO SEE MAP
ON PAGE 156

WAIMEA BAY
BEACH PARK

TO
HALEIWA

**PUPUKEA
BEACH PARK**

# Hike 26
# Kaunala Loop

Open to the public on weekends and holidays only.
Do not let the "Private Property—No Trespassing" signs stop you.
Staying on the road to the foot trail is permissible.

**Hiking distance:** 5 mile loop
**Hiking time:** 3 hours
**Elevation gain:** 900 feet
**Maps:** U.S.G.S. Waimea and Kahuku
Oahu Reference Maps: North Shore/Leeward Coast

**Summary of hike:** The Kaunala Trail, in the Pupukea Paumalu Forest Reserve, is a favorite hike with a wide cross section of natural features. The diverse hike includes lush tropical forests, jungle stream crossings, forested valleys, ridges, and sweeping ridgetop vistas of the mountains and coastline. The serpentine path winds through a forest canopy with groves of eucalyptus, ohia, kukui, ironwood, mahogany, silk, and Norfolk Island pine.

**Driving directions:** From Waikiki, take H-1 west for 16 miles to Exit 8, the H-2/Wahiawa exit. Drive 8 miles north on H-2 to Highway 99 in Wahiawa. Take Highway 99/Kamehameha Highway, north to the Weed Circle round-about, just south of Haleiwa. Take Highway 83, the Kamehameha Highway, a short distance into the town of Haleiwa. From Haleiwa, continue 5 miles northeast on Highway 83 to Foodland Market at Pupukea Road. Turn right on Pupukea Road, and drive until the public road ends at a gate with private property notices. Park off road near the gate.

**Hiking directions:** Hike to the end of the tree-lined public road to a locked military gate. Go around the gate past the hunter check-in booth. Follow the unpaved road for a half mile to a grove of paperbark trees. Watch for the signed Kaunala Trail on the left. Take the footpath and zigzag down the contours of the hillside to Paumalu Stream. Slowly climb up the hillside on the winding path to a jeep road on the ridge. Bear right and head uphill along the road. Follow the ridge to the high point of the hike—a flat clearing at 1,403 feet with panoramic vistas. Descend from the summit to a gate and cross over it, reaching a junction with the military access road. Go to the right and return on the main trail back to the trail-head.

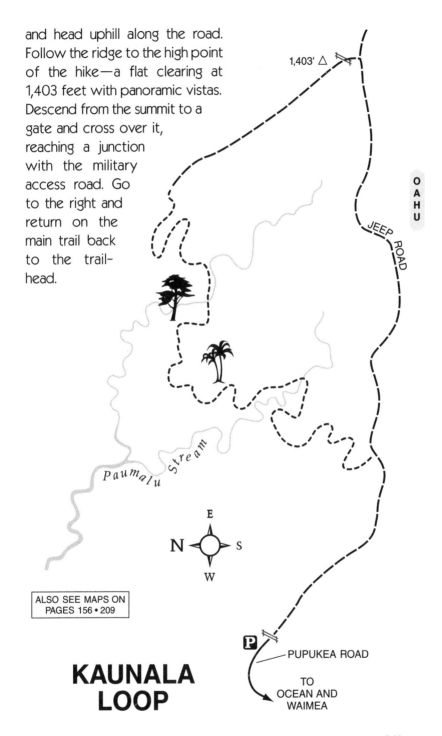

1,403' △

O
A
H
U

JEEP ROAD

Paumalu Stream

E
N ◇ S
W

ALSO SEE MAPS ON
PAGES 156 • 209

P

PUPUKEA ROAD

TO
OCEAN AND
WAIMEA

# KAUNALA LOOP

# Hike 27
# Hauula Loop Trail

**Hiking distance:** 2.5 mile loop
**Hiking time:** 1.5 hours
**Elevation gain:** 600 feet
**Maps:** U.S.G.S. Hauula
       Oahu Reference Maps: Central Oahu/Windward Coast

**Summary of hike:** The Hauula Loop Trail is a beautiful mountain hike in the Kaipapau Forest Reserve above Hauula. The trail crosses Waipilopilo Gulch and winds up the hillside through an ironwood, Norfolk Island pine, and paperback eucalyptus forest with lush fern and moss undergrowth. Fallen needles from the trees carpet the path with a thick matting. From the ridge are panoramic views of Kaipapau Valley, the Koolau Range, and the eastern coastline.

**Driving directions:** From Waikiki, take H-1 west 3.5 miles to Likelike Highway (63), and head northeast to the windward coast. After crossing the mountains, there are two driving options. The shorter, more direct route is the Kahekili Highway (83)—turn left (north) off the Likelike Highway at 7.5 miles. The more scenic but longer route is the Kamehameha Highway (836), a half mile further on the Likelike Highway (63). Both 83 and 836 merge together about 4.5 miles up the coast. (See map on page 157.) From this junction drive 15.5 miles northwest to Kukuna Road, between mile markers 21 and 22 in the town of Hauula. Turn left and take Kukuna Road to the stop sign. Turn right on Hauula Homestead Road 0.2 miles to Maakua Road. Turn left and park at the end of the street by the trail sign.

From the town of Haleiwa on the north shore, Kukuna Road is 19 miles northeast along Highway 83.

**Hiking directions:** Walk inland on the spur road to the trail sign. Cross the dry streambed to a trail junction about 70 yards ahead. The Maakua Gulch Trail and Papali–Maakua Ridge Trail (Hike 28) bear left. Take the right fork across the gulch, and gently climb up several switchbacks to a trail split. Begin the loop to the left, climbing up the hillside through dense, shady thickets to the ridge overlooking the canyons, mountains, and ocean. Descend into Waipilopilo Gulch, and cross the ravine to the next ridge overlooking Kaipapau Valley. Curve to the right, returning on the crest of the narrow ridge towards the ocean. Recross Waipilopilo Gulch and descend on switchbacks, completing the loop. Retrace your steps to the left.

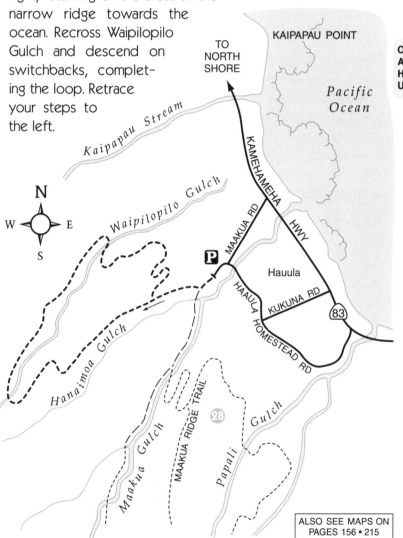

ALSO SEE MAPS ON
PAGES 156 • 215

# HAUULA LOOP TRAIL

# Hike 28
# Maakua Ridge Trail and Papali Gulch

**Hiking distance:** 3 mile loop
**Hiking time:** 1.5 hours
**Elevation gain:** 800 feet
**Maps:** U.S.G.S. Hauula
   Oahu Reference Maps: Central Oahu/Windward Coast

**Summary of hike:** The Maakua Ridge Trail sits above the town of Hauula in the Kaipapau Forest Reserve. The trail begins in Maakua Gulch and crosses over Maakua Ridge into Papali Gulch, forming a loop. The forested path winds through lush groves of hau, Norfolk Island pines, hala, acacia, and kukui trees with a lush understory of ferns and mosses. From the ridge are vistas of the Koolau Range, Maakua Gulch, the surrounding countryside, and the windward coast.

**Driving directions:** Follow the driving directions for Hike 27.

**Hiking directions:** Walk inland on the spur road to the trail sign. Cross the dry streambed to a junction about 70 yards ahead. The Hauula Trail (Hike 27) bears right. Stay in Maakua Gulch on the old road to the left about 200 yards to a posted junction. Bear left on the Maakua Ridge Trail, crossing Maakua Gulch. Switchbacks lead up the hillside to a trail split. Begin the loop to the right, climbing to the ridgeline. Descend into Papali Gulch and cross the stream. Curve left, gradually ascending the hillside to the next ridge. Return to the north and traverse the shady slopes above Punaiki Gulch. Zigzag down the hill and recross Papali Gulch. Curve inland, climbing out of the gulch and completing the loop. Retrace your steps to the right.

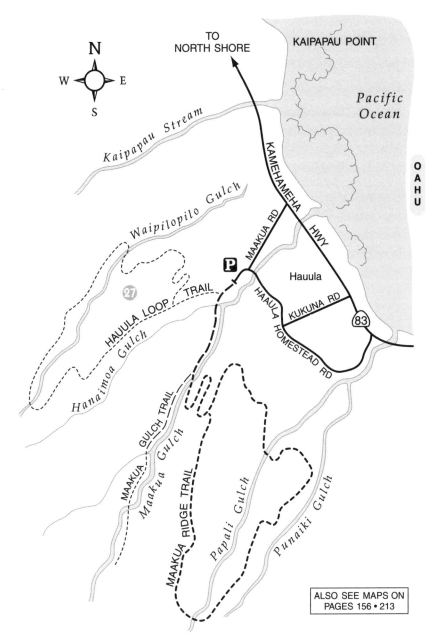

# MAAKUA RIDGE TRAIL
## PAPALI GULCH

# Hike 29
# Kapaeleele Koa and Keaniani Kilo Lookouts
## KAHANA VALLEY STATE PARK

**Hiking distance:** 1.2 mile loop
**Hiking time:** 45 minutes
**Elevation gain:** 150 feet
**Maps:** U.S.G.S. Kahana
 Oahu Reference Maps: Central Oahu/Windward Coast

**Summary of hike:** This short loop hike leads to Kapaeleele Koa and Keaniani Kilo, two ancient Hawaiian fishing shrines on the oceanfront cliffs high above Kahana Bay. The trail, maintained by the local Boy Scouts, is at the mouth of Kahana Valley and returns along the sandy shoreline in Kahana Bay.

**Driving directions:** From Waikiki, take H-1 west 3.5 miles to Likelike Highway (63), and head northeast to the windward coast. After crossing the mountains, there are two driving options. The shorter, more direct route is the Kahekili Highway (83)—turn left (north) off the Likelike Highway at 7.5 miles. The more scenic but longer route is the Kamehameha Highway (836), a half mile further on the Likelike Highway (63). Both 83 and 836 merge together about 4.5 miles up the coast. (See map on page 157.) From this junction drive 10.2 miles northwest on Highway 83 to Kahana Bay between mile markers 25 and 26. Turn left at the Kahana Valley State Park sign. Park by the orientation center on the right.

 From the town of Haleiwa on the north shore, Kahana Bay is 24.3 miles northeast along Highway 83.

**Hiking directions:** Walk past the orientation center on the grassy path to the posted Kapaeleele Trailhead. Head into the forest and begin climbing the cliffs along the base of Puu Piei to vistas across Kahana Bay. The path reaches Kapaeleele Koa, a fenced shrine with offerings where fishermen pray for a good catch. Continue traversing the hillside to a posted T-junction. Take the left fork for a short, steep detour to Keaniani Kilo, which means "sparkling lookout." From this fenced shrine are fantastic views of the bay. Return to the main trail, and continue the loop to the left, zigzagging down the steep cliff to a ditch near the highway. Cross the highway and bear right on the sandy beach in Kahana Bay. Recross the highway at the state park entrance, returning to the parking lot.

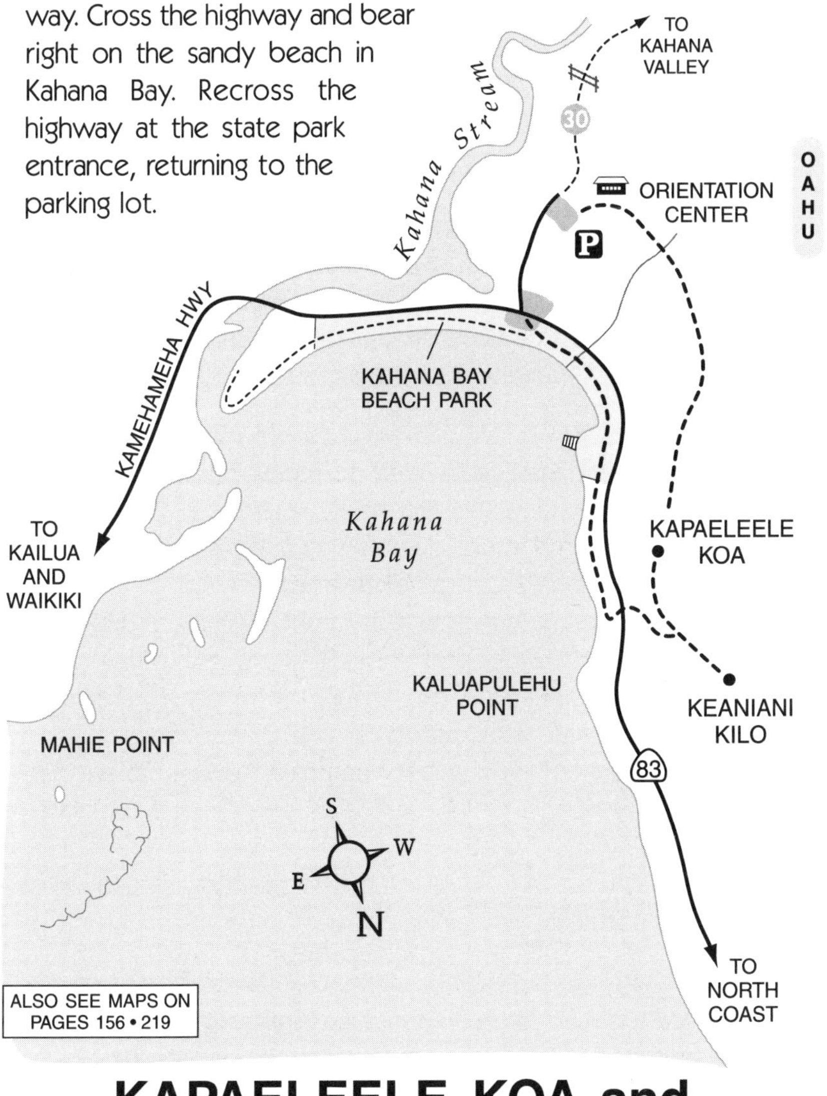

TO KAHANA VALLEY

Kahana Stream

30

ORIENTATION CENTER

P

O A H U

KAMEHAMEHA HWY

KAHANA BAY BEACH PARK

TO KAILUA AND WAIKIKI

*Kahana Bay*

KAPAELEELE KOA

KALUAPULEHU POINT

KEANIANI KILO

MAHIE POINT

83

S

W

E

N

TO NORTH COAST

ALSO SEE MAPS ON PAGES 156 • 219

# KAPAELEELE KOA and KEANIANI KILO LOOKOUTS
## KAHANA VALLEY STATE PARK

# Hike 30
# Nakoa Trail
## KAHANA VALLEY STATE PARK

**Hiking distance:** 5 mile loop
**Hiking time:** 3 hours
**Elevation gain:** 300 feet
**Maps:** U.S.G.S. Kahana
Oahu Reference Maps: Central Oahu/Windward Coast

**Summary of hike:** The Nakoa Trail, located in Kahana Valley State Park, leads through a lush vegetated rainforest to a large and deep swimming hole by a dam. The wildland valley is among the wettest valleys on Oahu, with as much as 300 inches of rain annually. Kahana Stream flows from the Koolau Mountains through the valley and empties into Kahana Bay.

**Driving directions:** Follow the driving directions for Hike 29.

**Hiking directions:** From the Orientation Center, follow the main road up Kahana Valley, passing residential homes and covered shelters. Go around a locked vehicle-restricted gate to a road split. Stay to the right on the main road, reaching another junction by a hunter check-in station at 1.25 miles. The left fork leads directly to the pool. Take the right fork and begin the loop, passing through another locked gate to a water tank. Follow the contours of the hillside, with sweeping views of Kahana Valley and the bay. Cross two small tributary streams to a junction just before reaching Kahana Stream. Bear left, then descend and cross Kahana Stream. At the next junction, take a sharp left. Descend from the ridge along the terraced slopes to the pool at Kahana Stream. Cross the small dam to complete the loop. Take the road to the right, back to the parking lot.

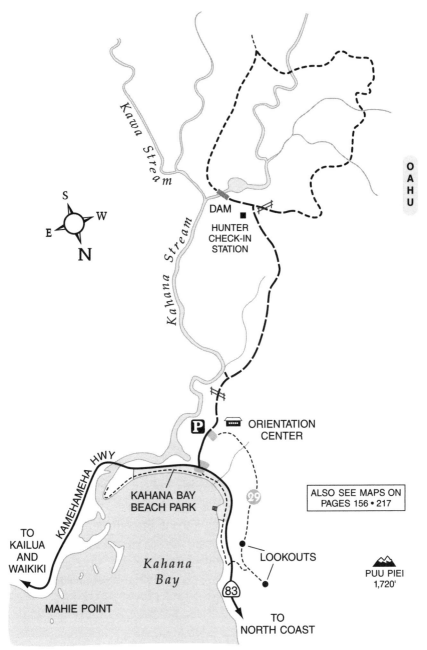

**OAHU**

*Kawa Stream*

*Kahana Stream*

DAM

HUNTER
CHECK-IN
STATION

**P**  ORIENTATION
CENTER

KAMEHAMEHA HWY

KAHANA BAY
BEACH PARK

29

ALSO SEE MAPS ON
PAGES 156 • 217

TO
KAILUA
AND
WAIKIKI

*Kahana
Bay*

LOOKOUTS

PUU PIEI
1,720'

MAHIE POINT

83

TO
NORTH COAST

# NAKOA TRAIL
## KAHANA VALLEY STATE PARK

# DAY HIKE BOOKS

| | | |
|---|---|---|
| Day Hikes On the California Central Coast | 1-57342-031-X | $14.95 |
| Day Hikes On the California Southern Coast | 1-57342-045-X | 14.95 |
| Day Hikes Around Monterey and Carmel | 1-57342-036-0 | 14.95 |
| Day Hikes Around Big Sur | 1-57342-041-7 | 14.95 |
| Day Hikes Around San Luis Obispo | 1-57342-051-4 | 16.95 |
| Day Hikes Around Santa Barbara | 1-57342-042-5 | 14.95 |
| Day Hikes Around Ventura County | 1-57342-043-3 | 14.95 |
| Day Hikes Around Los Angeles | 1-57342-044-1 | 14.95 |
| Day Hikes Around Orange County | 1-57342-047-6 | 15.95 |
| Day Hikes In Yosemite National Park | 1-57342-037-9 | 11.95 |
| Day Hikes In Sequoia and Kings Canyon Nat'l. Parks | 1-57342-030-1 | 12.95 |
| Day Hikes Around Sedona, Arizona | 1-57342-049-2 | 14.95 |
| Day Hikes On Oahu | 1-57342-038-7 | 11.95 |
| Day Hikes On Maui | 1-57342-039-5 | 11.95 |
| Day Hikes On Kauai | 1-57342-040-9 | 11.95 |
| Day Hikes In Hawaii | 1-57342-050-6 | 16.95 |
| Day Hikes In Yellowstone National Park | 1-57342-048-4 | 12.95 |
| Day Hikes In Grand Teton National Park | 1-57342-046-8 | 11.95 |
| Day Hikes In the Beartooth Mountains Red Lodge, MT to Yellowstone Nat'l. Park | 1-57342-052-2 | 13.95 |
| Day Hikes Around Bozeman, Montana | 1-57342-033-6 | 11.95 |
| Day Hikes Around Missoula, Montana | 1-57342-032-8 | 11.95 |

**DAY HIKES ON THE**
### California Central Coast

71 GREAT HIKES
Robert Stone

**DAY HIKES ON THE**
### California Southern Coast

100 GREAT HIKES
Robert Stone

**DAY HIKES AROUND**
### Monterey & Carmel

77 GREAT HIKES
Robert Stone

**DAY HIKES AROUND**
### Big Sur

80 GREAT HIKES
Robert Stone

**DAY HIKES AROUND**
### San Luis Obispo

Robert Stone
2nd EDITION

**DAY HIKES AROUND**
### Santa Barbara

82 GREAT HIKES
Robert Stone
3rd EDITION

**DAY HIKES AROUND**
### Ventura County

82 GREAT HIKES
Robert Stone
2nd EDITION

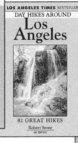

**LOS ANGELES TIMES BESTSELLER**
**DAY HIKES AROUND**
### Los Angeles

82 GREAT HIKES
Robert Stone
4th EDITION

**DAY HIKES AROUND**
### Orange County

108 GREAT HIKES
Robert Stone

**DAY HIKES IN**
### Yosemite NATIONAL PARK

55 GREAT HIKES
Robert Stone
3rd EDITION

**DAY HIKES IN**
### Sequoia & Kings Canyon NATIONAL PARKS

Robert Stone

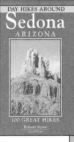

**DAY HIKES AROUND**
### Sedona ARIZONA

100 GREAT HIKES
Robert Stone
2nd EDITION

**DAY HIKES ON**
### Oahu

57 GREAT HIKES
Robert Stone
3rd EDITION

**DAY HIKES ON**
### Maui

55 GREAT HIKES
Robert Stone
3rd EDITION

**DAY HIKES ON**
### Kauai

55 GREAT HIKES
Robert Stone
2nd EDITION

**DAY HIKES IN**
### Yellowstone NATIONAL PARK

82 GREAT HIKES
Robert Stone
4th EDITION

**DAY HIKES IN**
### Grand Teton NATIONAL PARK

72 GREAT HIKES
Robert Stone
4th EDITION

**DAY HIKES IN THE**
### Beartooth Mountains

FROM BILLINGS TO RED LODGE TO YELLOWSTONE NATIONAL PARK
Robert Stone
4th EDITION

**DAY HIKES AROUND**
### Bozeman MONTANA

INCLUDING THE GALLATIN CANYON AND PARADISE VALLEY
Robert Stone
2nd EDITION

**DAY HIKES AROUND**
### Missoula MONTANA

INCLUDING THE BITTERROOT AND THE SEELEY-SWAN VALLEY
Robert Stone
2nd EDITION

# Notes

## About the Author

Since 1991, veteran hiker Robert Stone has been writer, photographer, and publisher of Day Hike Books. Robert has hiked every trail in the *Day Hike Book* series. With 21 hiking guides in the series, many in their second, third, and fourth editions, he has hiked thousands of miles of trails throughout the western United States and Hawaii. When Robert is not hiking, he researches, writes, and maps the hikes before returning to the trails. He is an active member of RMOWP (Rocky Mountain Outdoor Writers and Photographers), OWAC (Outdoor Writers Associaton of California), and a Los Angeles Times Best Selling Author. Robert spends summers in the Rocky Mountains of Montana and winters on the California Central Coast.